FIRST NAME _____ SURNAME _____

HOME ADDRESS (LINE 1) _____

HOME ADDRESS (LINE 2) _____

HOME PHONE _____ MOBILE PHONE _____

EMAIL _____

TWITTER _____ INSTAGRAM _____

BUSINESS/COLLEGE ADDRESS (LINE 1) _____

BUSINESS/COLLEGE ADDRESS (LINE 2) _____

BUSINESS/COLLEGE PHONE _____ BUSINESS/COLLEGE EMAIL _____

EMERGENCY CONTACT (NAME AND PHONE NUMBER) _____

BLOOD GROUP _____

ALLERGIES _____

VACCINATIONS _____

UK BANK HOLIDAYS

JANUARY 3RD — Substitute for New Year's Day

APRIL 15TH — Good Friday

APRIL 18TH — Easter Monday

MAY 2ND — Early May Bank Holiday

JUNE 2ND — Spring Bank Holiday

JUNE 3RD — Platinum Jubilee Bank Holiday

AUGUST 29TH — Summer Bank Holiday

DECEMBER 26TH — Boxing Day

DECEMBER 27TH — Substitute for Christmas Day

US FEDERAL HOLIDAYS

JANUARY 1ST — New Year's Day

JANUARY 17TH — Martin Luther King Day

FEBRUARY 21ST — Presidents' Day

MAY 30TH — Memorial Day

JULY 4TH — Independence Day

SEPTEMBER 5TH — Labor Day

OCTOBER 10TH — Indigenous Peoples' Day

NOVEMBER 11TH — Veterans Day

NOVEMBER 24TH — Thanksgiving

DECEMBER 26TH — Substitute for Christmas Day

Verso Books is the largest independent,
radical publishing house in the English-speaking world.

Launched by *New Left Review* in 1970, Verso
is a leading publisher in current affairs, philosophy,
history, politics and economics.

"A rigorously intelligent publisher."
—*SUNDAY TIMES*

"Anglo-America's preeminent radical press."
—*HARPER'S*

VERSOBOOKS.COM

Buy securely and easily from our website—
great discounts, free shipping with a minimum order
and a free ebook bundled with many of our hard-copy books.

Check our website to read our blog and see our
latest titles—featuring essays, videos, podcasts,
interviews with authors, news, exclusive competitions
and details of forthcoming events.

Sign up to our email list to be the first to hear of
our new titles, special offers and events.

Verso Books   @VersoBooks   versobooks

Some of the quotes in the calendar are drawn
from *The Verso Book of Dissent*, edited by
Andrew Hsiao and Audrea Lim (Verso 2020).

2022

JANUARY

S	M	T	W	TH	F	S
26	27	28	29	30	31	1
2	3	4	5	6	7	8
9	10	11	12	13	14	15
16	17	18	19	20	21	22
23	24	25	26	27	28	29
30	31					

FEBRUARY

S	M	T	W	TH	F	S
30	31	1	2	3	4	5
6	7	8	9	10	11	12
13	14	15	16	17	18	19
20	21	22	23	24	25	26
27	28	1	2	3	4	5

MARCH

S	M	T	W	TH	F	S
27	28	1	2	3	4	5
6	7	8	9	10	11	12
13	14	15	16	17	18	19
20	21	22	23	24	25	26
27	28	29	30	31	1	2

APRIL

S	M	T	W	TH	F	S
27	28	29	30	31	1	2
3	4	5	6	7	8	9
10	11	12	13	14	15	16
17	18	19	20	21	22	23
24	25	26	27	28	29	30

MAY

S	M	T	W	TH	F	S
1	2	3	4	5	6	7
8	9	10	11	12	13	14
15	16	17	18	19	20	21
22	23	24	25	26	27	28
29	30	31	1	2	3	4

JUNE

S	M	T	W	TH	F	S
29	30	31	1	2	3	4
5	6	7	8	9	10	11
12	13	14	15	16	17	18
19	20	21	22	23	24	25
26	27	28	29	30	1	2

JULY

S	M	T	W	TH	F	S
26	27	28	29	30	1	2
3	4	5	6	7	8	9
10	11	12	13	14	15	16
17	18	19	20	21	22	23
24	25	26	27	28	29	30
31						

AUGUST

S	M	T	W	TH	F	S
31	1	2	3	4	5	6
7	8	9	10	11	12	13
14	15	16	17	18	19	20
21	22	23	24	25	26	27
28	29	30	31	1	2	3

SEPTEMBER

S	M	T	W	TH	F	S
28	29	30	31	1	2	3
4	5	6	7	8	9	10
11	12	13	14	15	16	17
18	19	20	21	22	23	24
25	26	27	28	29	30	1

OCTOBER

S	M	T	W	TH	F	S
25	26	27	28	29	30	1
2	3	4	5	6	7	8
9	10	11	12	13	14	15
16	17	18	19	20	21	22
23	24	25	26	27	28	29
30	31					

NOVEMBER

S	M	T	W	TH	F	S
30	31	1	2	3	4	5
6	7	8	9	10	11	12
13	14	15	16	17	18	19
20	21	22	23	24	25	26
27	28	29	30	1	2	3

DECEMBER

S	M	T	W	TH	F	S
27	28	29	30	1	2	3
4	5	6	7	8	9	10
11	12	13	14	15	16	17
18	19	20	21	22	23	24
25	26	27	28	29	30	31

2023

JANUARY

S	M	T	W	TH	F	S
1	2	3	4	5	6	7
8	9	10	11	12	13	14
15	16	17	18	19	20	21
22	23	24	25	26	27	28
29	30	31	1	2	3	4

FEBRUARY

S	M	T	W	TH	F	S
29	30	31	1	2	3	4
5	6	7	8	9	10	11
12	13	14	15	16	17	18
19	20	21	22	23	24	25
26	27	28	1	2	3	4

MARCH

S	M	T	W	TH	F	S
26	27	28	1	2	3	4
5	6	7	8	9	10	11
12	13	14	15	16	17	18
19	20	21	22	23	24	25
26	27	28	29	30	31	1

APRIL

S	M	T	W	TH	F	S
26	27	28	29	30	31	1
2	3	4	5	6	7	8
9	10	11	12	13	14	15
16	17	18	19	20	21	22
23	24	25	26	27	28	29
30						

MAY

S	M	T	W	TH	F	S
30	1	2	3	4	5	6
7	8	9	10	11	12	13
14	15	16	17	18	19	20
21	22	23	24	25	26	27
28	29	30	31	1	2	3

JUNE

S	M	T	W	TH	F	S
28	29	30	31	1	2	3
4	5	6	7	8	9	10
11	12	13	14	15	16	17
18	19	20	21	22	23	24
25	26	27	28	29	30	1

JULY

S	M	T	W	TH	F	S
25	26	27	28	29	30	1
2	3	4	5	6	7	8
9	10	11	12	13	14	15
16	17	18	19	20	21	22
23	24	25	26	27	28	29
30	31					

AUGUST

S	M	T	W	TH	F	S
30	31	1	2	3	4	5
6	7	8	9	10	11	12
13	14	15	16	17	18	19
20	21	22	23	24	25	26
27	28	29	30	31	1	2

SEPTEMBER

S	M	T	W	TH	F	S
27	28	29	30	31	1	2
3	4	5	6	7	8	9
10	11	12	13	14	15	16
17	18	19	20	21	22	23
24	25	26	27	28	29	30

OCTOBER

S	M	T	W	TH	F	S
1	2	3	4	5	6	7
8	9	10	11	12	13	14
15	16	17	18	19	20	21
22	23	24	25	26	27	28
29	30	31	1	2	3	4

NOVEMBER

S	M	T	W	TH	F	S
29	30	31	1	2	3	4
5	6	7	8	9	10	11
12	13	14	15	16	17	18
19	20	21	22	23	24	25
26	27	28	29	30	1	2

DECEMBER

S	M	T	W	TH	F	S
26	27	28	29	30	1	2
3	4	5	6	7	8	9
10	11	12	13	14	15	16
17	18	19	20	21	22	23
24	25	26	27	28	29	30
31						

VERSO CLASSICS: A READING LIST

Verso—the left-hand page—has been publishing landmark radical books for over 50 years, by thinkers including Tariq Ali, Walter Benjamin, Ellen Meiksins Wood, Perry Anderson, Angela Davis, Judith Butler, Theodor Adorno, and many more. In this reading list we bring you a selection of books from across our publishing; a starting place for exploring 50 years of radical ideas.

VERSO BOOK OF DISSENT
ANDY HSIAO AND AUDREA LIM

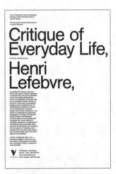

CRITIQUE OF EVERYDAY LIFE
HENRI LEFEBVRE

THE FORCE OF NONVIOLENCE
JUDITH BUTLER

REVOLTING PROSTITUTES
JUNO MAC AND MOLLY SMITH

I, RIGOBERTA MENCHÚ:
AN INDIAN WOMAN IN GUATEMALA
RIGOBERTA MENCHÚ

THE VERSO BOOK OF FEMINISM:
REVOLUTIONARY WORDS FROM FOUR
MILLENNIA OF REBELLION
EDITED BY JESSIE KINDIG

CONSIDERATIONS ON WESTERN MARXISM
PERRY ANDERSON

READING CAPITAL
LOUIS ALTHUSSER AND ETIENNE BALIBAR

POSTMODERNISM, OR,
THE CULTURAL LOGIC OF LATE CAPITALISM
FREDRIC JAMESON

MINIMA MORALIA:
REFLECTIONS FROM DAMAGED LIFE
THEODOR ADORNO

INVENTING THE FUTURE: POSTCAPITALISM
AND A WORLD WITHOUT WORK
NICK SRNICEK AND ALEX WILLIAMS

THE COMPLETE WORKS OF
ROSA LUXEMBURG,
VOLUME I: ECONOMIC WRITINGS 1
ROSA LUXEMBURG

THE SUBLIME OBJECT OF IDEOLOGY
SLAVOJ ŽIŽEK

IMAGINED COMMUNITIES
BENEDICT ANDERSON

CHAVS: THE DEMONIZATION OF THE
WORKING CLASS
OWEN JONES

IF THEY COME IN THE MORNING...:
VOICES OF RESISTANCE
EDITED BY ANGELA Y. DAVIS

THE ORIGIN OF CAPITALISM
ELLEN MEIKSINS WOOD

AUTOMATION AND
THE FUTURE OF WORK
AARON BENANAV

A PLANET TO WIN:
WHY WE NEED A GREEN NEW DEAL
KATE ARONOFF,
ALYSSA BATTISTONI, ET AL.

AESTHETICS AND POLITICS
THEODOR ADORNO,
WALTER BENJAMIN, ET AL.

MISTAKEN IDENTITY:
RACE AND CLASS IN THE AGE OF TRUMP
ASAD HAIDER

RED ROSA: A GRAPHIC BIOGRAPHY
OF ROSA LUXEMBURG
KATE EVANS

ARTIFICIAL HELLS: PARTICIPATORY ART
AND THE POLITICS OF SPECTATORSHIP
CLAIRE BISHOP

THE LEFT HEMISPHERE:
MAPPING CRITICAL THEORY TODAY
RAZMIG KEUCHEYAN

FORTUNES OF FEMINISM:
FROM STATE-MANAGED CAPITALISM
TO NEOLIBERAL CRISIS
NANCY FRASER

PORTRAITS: JOHN BERGER ON ARTISTS
JOHN BERGER

PLANET OF SLUMS
MIKE DAVIS

INSURGENT EMPIRE
PRIYAMVADA GOPAL

SUNDAY DECEMBER 26

_____

_____

_____

_____

_____

_____

_____

MONDAY DECEMBER 27

_____

_____

_____

_____

_____

_____

_____

TUESDAY DECEMBER 28

_____

_____

_____

_____

_____

_____

_____

JANUARY 1, 1970 Gil Scott-Heron, the poet and recording artist who became a voice of black protest culture, releases his album _Small Talk at 125th and Lenox_, whose opening track is, "The Revolution Will Not be Televised."

"The revolution will not make you look five pounds thinner,
the revolution will not be televised, Brother."

JANUARY 1, 1994 Zapatista forces overtake towns in Chiapas, beginning an ongoing revolution against the Mexican state. "The dispossessed, we are millions, and we thereby call upon our brothers and sisters to join this struggle as the only path."
—ZAPATISTA ARMY OF NATIONAL LIBERATION

JANUARY 1, 2009 Oscar Grant III was a twenty-two-year-old black man, fatally shot by an Oakland, California, transit cop in the early morning hours of the New Year. The riots that followed were some of the largest the United States had seen in decades. "Oscar Grant: Murdered. The Whole Damn System Is Guilty!"
—PLACARD FROM THE OSCAR GRANT REBELLION

WEDNESDAY DECEMBER 29

Subcomandante Marcos and Comandante Tacho in La Realidad, Chiapas, 1999

THURSDAY DECEMBER 30

NOTES:

FRIDAY DECEMBER 31

SATURDAY JANUARY 1

SUNDAY JANUARY 2

_____

_____

_____

_____

_____

_____

_____

_____

MONDAY JANUARY 3

_____

_____

_____

_____

_____

_____

_____

TUESDAY JANUARY 4

_____

_____

_____

_____

_____

_____

_____

JANUARY 3, 1961 Angolan peasants employed by the Portuguese-Belgium cotton plantation company Cotonang begin protests over poor working conditions, setting off the Angolan struggle for independence from Portugal.

> "Tomorrow we will sing songs of freedom when we commemorate
> the day this slavery ends."
>
> —FIRST PRESIDENT OF ANGOLA AND LEADER OF THE MOVEMENT FOR THE LIBERATION OF ANGOLA ANTONIO AGOSTINHO NETO, "FAREWELL AT THE HOUR OF PARTING"

JANUARY 5, 1971 Angela Davis—black feminist, philosopher, and prison abolitionist—declares her innocence in a California court over the kidnapping and murder of a judge. "Prisons do not disappear problems, they disappear human beings. And the practice of disappearing vast numbers of people from poor, immigrant, and racially marginalized communities has literally become big business."
—"MASKED RACISM"

JANUARY 6, 1977 Charter 77, a document criticizing the Czech government for its human rights record, is published; it is violently suppressed.

JANUARY 7, 1957 Djamila Bouhired, the "Arab Joan of Arc" and member of the National Liberation Front, sets off a bomb in an Algiers café, precipitating the Battle of Algiers, a pivotal episode in the Algerian struggle for independence against the French. "It was the most beautiful day of my life because I was confident that I was going to be dying for the sake of the most wonderful story in the world."

WEDNESDAY JANUARY 5

_____

_____

_____

_____

_____

_____

_____

Rigoberta Menchú Tum, indigenous revolutionary and Nobel
Peace Prize winner

THURSDAY JANUARY 6

_____

_____

_____

_____

_____

_____

_____

NOTES:

_____

_____

_____

_____

_____

_____

FRIDAY JANUARY 7

_____

_____

_____

_____

_____

_____

SATURDAY JANUARY 8

_____

_____

_____

_____

_____

_____

SUNDAY JANUARY 9

_____
_____
_____
_____
_____
_____
_____
_____
_____

MONDAY JANUARY 10

_____
_____
_____
_____
_____
_____
_____

TUESDAY JANUARY 11

_____
_____
_____
_____
_____
_____
_____
_____

JANUARY 9, 1959 Rigoberta Menchú Tum, indigenous revolutionary and Nobel Peace Prize winner, is born in Chimel, Guatemala. "[My cause] wasn't born out of something good, it was born out of wretchedness and bitterness. It has been radicalized by the poverty in which my people live." —I, RIGOBERTA MENCHÚ

JANUARY 10, 1776 Thomas Paine, who participated in the American and French revolutions, publishes the pamphlet *Common Sense*, which argued for American independence from Britain. "Society in every state is a blessing, but government even in its best state is but a necessary evil; in its worst state an intolerable one."

JANUARY 11, 1894 Donghak Rebellion begins in Mujiang, Korea, over local corruption, eventually growing into an anti-establishment movement. "The people are the root of the nation. If the root withers, the nation will be enfeebled." —DONGHAK REBELLION PROCLAMATION

JANUARY 11, 1912 Workers in Lawrence, Massachusetts, walk out over a race-based pay cut in what would become known as the "bread and roses" strike. Soon an Industrial Workers of the World–organized strike shuts down every textile mill in the city.

JANUARY 15, 1919 Rosa Luxemburg, founder of the Spartacus League, is murdered by the German Social Democratic government. "The madness will cease and the bloody demons of hell will vanish only when workers in Germany and France, England and Russia finally awake from their stupor, extend to each other a brotherly hand, and drown out the bestial chorus of imperialist war-mongers." —JUNIUS PAMPHLET

WEDNESDAY JANUARY 12

Strikers face the Massachusetts State Militia, 1912

THURSDAY JANUARY 13

NOTES:

FRIDAY JANUARY 14

SATURDAY JANUARY 15

SUNDAY JANUARY 16

MONDAY JANUARY 17

TUESDAY JANUARY 18

JANUARY 17, 1893 Queen Lili'uokalani, Hawaii's last monarch, is overthrown by American colonists.

JANUARY 17, 1961 Patrice Lumumba, Congolese independence leader and first prime minister of independent Congo, is assassinated by the Belgian government. Six months earlier, he had been deposed in a CIA-backed coup. "They are trying to distort your focus when they call our government a communist government, in the pay of the Soviet Union, or say that Lumumba is a communist, an anti-white: Lumumba is an African."

JANUARY 20, 1973 Amílcar Cabral, a communist intellectual and guerrilla leader of Guinea-Bissau's anti-colonial movement against the Portuguese, is assassinated. Guinea-Bissau became independent just months later. "Honesty, in a political context, is total commitment and total identification with the toiling masses."

JANUARY 20, 2017 Hundreds of protesters are arrested in Washington, DC as Donald Trump is inaugurated as US president, and the following day, an estimated 470,000 people rally for the Women's March on Washington. "Pussy Grabs Back." —PROTEST SLOGAN

JANUARY 21, 1935 The Wilderness Society is founded by conservationists; it would become one of the most radical US environmentalist groups into the 1970s. "Our bigger-and-better society is now like a hypochondriac, so obsessed with its own economic health as to have lost the capacity to remain healthy." —SOCIETY FOUNDER ALDO LEOPOLD, *A SAND COUNTY ALMANAC*

WEDNESDAY JANUARY 19

_____
_____
_____
_____
_____
_____
_____

Patrice Lumumba (1925-1961) raises his unshackled arms
following his release, 1960

THURSDAY JANUARY 20

_____
_____
_____
_____
_____
_____
_____

NOTES:

_____
_____
_____
_____
_____
_____

FRIDAY JANUARY 21

_____
_____
_____
_____
_____
_____

SATURDAY JANUARY 22

_____
_____
_____
_____
_____
_____

ART AND MUSEUMS IN AN AGE OF PROTEST
LAURA RAICOVICH

We are living in an age of protest. Around the globe, radical movements, from prison and debt abolition to Extinction Rebellion's climate activism, have penetrated mainstream discourse. Culture and art have, necessarily, also come under fire. While art has enormous potential to shift society, the institutions upon which it relies help hold systems of power in place. As much as I love museums and have dedicated my career to them, they are repositories of cultural hegemony, mirrors of society's ills, from enormous wealth gaps and other legacies of colonialism to the exclusion of historically marginalized groups. Museums and cultural spaces are part of the systems that protests hope to undo. I believe this undoing and redoing can not only make museums better for more people, but also map ways to make change in society at large.

Over the past several years, protests have erupted regularly around how museums are funded, how they are organized, what they show and how, who holds power within their structures, and how they reflect, or fail to reflect, a whole diversity of identities. In this book I examine examples of these protests or calls for accountability in order to delve into both the histories of museums and cultural institutions in the United States, and the useful lessons that might emerge; these constitute fascinating and revealing entry points to the manifestation of coloniality, white supremacy, class bias, and innumerable other social dimensions that persist and are contested today.

As publics increase their demands for greater agency, inclusion, and diversity, cultural spaces must examine their own ways of being in order to remain relevant. I believe that to address the inequities that continue

to haunt our institutions, and indeed society, we could not find a better place to begin than by dismantling the myth of neutrality in our cultural spaces.

This question of whether museums are neutral, then, is the crux of a contemporary conundrum about how stories have been told, who has told them, why and how they have been framed and historicized, and what it means that foundational stories are being challenged today by a whole diversity of perspectives. Some of these perspectives, it must be noted, have been marginalized from society for their race, gender identity, class, educational levels, ability, etc., throughout many decades. Since museums are the West's mode of preserving history, we then must ask, has the museum ever really been a neutral space?

At a moment in human history when we must contemplate our own potential extinction due to extreme climate conditions we have brought about, and when the rise of nationalism and xenophobia internationally has reared its head yet again in increasingly virulent and violent ways, how does culture respond? And how do museums remain relevant in such times, especially when various publics and foundations are calling on museums to be publicly accountable for the ways in which they make decisions and for the ways they work? It is in this context, and at this urgent moment, that I believe we must be able to identify the biases of our museums, to understand the worldviews they both promote and marginalize, and to interrogate these ways of being, working, organizing, and making culture.

This is a revised extract from Culture Strike: Art and Museums in an Age of Protest *by Laura Raicovich (Verso, 2021).*

JANUARY 23, 1976 Paul Robeson, the African-American singer and civil rights campaigner, dies. "I stand always on the side of those who will toil and labor. As an artist I come to sing, but as a citizen, I will always speak for peace, and no one can silence me in this."

JANUARY 24, 1911 The anarcho-feminist Kanno Sugako is hanged for plotting to assassinate Emperor Meiji. "In accordance with long-standing customs, we have been seen as a form of material property. Women in Japan are in a state of slavery."
—"WOMEN ARE SLAVES"

JANUARY 27, 1924 Lenin's funeral takes place in Red Square. In attendance was the poet Vladimir Mayakovsky, who went on to pen the epic poem, "Vladimir Ilyich Lenin."

"Just guzzling
        snoozing
                and pocketing pelf,
Capitalism
        got lazy and feeble."

JANUARY 28, 1948 A plane crash kills twenty-eight bracero farm workers being sent back to Mexico. Cesar Chavez considered the moment part of his early political education.

"Who are all these friends, all scattered like dry leaves?
The radio says, 'They are just deportees ...'"
—WOODY GUTHRIE, "DEPORTEE"

JANUARY 29, 1967 Arusha Declaration, written by Julius Nyerere, is issued to clarify Tanzania's path toward Ujamaa, or African socialism. "We, in Africa, have no more need of being 'converted' to socialism than we have of being 'taught' democracy."
—"UJAMAA, THE BASIS OF AFRICAN SOCIALISM"

WEDNESDAY JANUARY 26

The 35th Bloody Sunday memorial march in Derry, 28 January 2007

THURSDAY JANUARY 27

NOTES:

FRIDAY JANUARY 28

SATURDAY JANUARY 29

SUNDAY JANUARY 30

_____

_____

_____

_____

_____

_____

MONDAY JANUARY 31

_____

_____

_____

_____

_____

_____

TUESDAY FEBRUARY 1

_____

_____

_____

_____

_____

_____

_____

JANUARY 30, 1972 British soldiers shot twenty-eight unarmed civilians in Northern Ireland during a peaceful protest march against internment, in what become known as Bloody Sunday—one of the most significant brutal events of The Troubles.

FEBRUARY 1, 1902 Langston Hughes, poet and figure of the Harlem Renaissance, is born.

"What happens to a dream deferred?
Does it dry up
like a raisin in the sun?
Or fester like a sore—
and then run?"
—"MONTAGE OF A DREAM DEFERRED"

FEBRUARY 2, 1512 Taíno hero Hatuey is captured and killed after besieging the Spaniards for four months at their first fort in Cuba. "[Gold] is the God the Spaniards worship. For these they fight and kill, for these they persecute us and that is why we have to throw them into the sea." —HATUEY'S SPEECH TO THE TAÍNOS

FEBRUARY 3, 1930 The Indochinese Communist Party is established; it conducted an underground struggle against the French colonialists and, later, the American invaders.

FEBRUARY 4, 1899 Philippine-American war begins after the Philippine government objects to being handed over to the US from Spain.

"The North
Americans have
captured nothing
but a vessel
of water,
nothing that
our sun
will find difficult
to empty with its rage."
—ALFREDO NAVARRO SALANGA

WEDNESDAY FEBRUARY 2

Torture of Hatuey in Cuba, by Theodor de Bry, 1590

THURSDAY FEBRUARY 3

NOTES:

FRIDAY FEBRUARY 4

SATURDAY FEBRUARY 5

SUNDAY FEBRUARY 6

_____

_____

_____

_____

_____

_____

_____

_____

MONDAY FEBRUARY 7

_____

_____

_____

_____

_____

_____

TUESDAY FEBRUARY 8

_____

_____

_____

_____

_____

_____

_____

FEBRUARY 7, 1948 Tens of thousands of silent marchers in Bogotá memorialize victims of Colombian state violence. "Señor Presidente, our flag is in mourning; this silent multitude, the mute cry from our hearts, asks only that you treat us ... as you would have us treat you." —JORGE ELIÉCER GAITÁN, LEADER OF THE COLOMBIAN LIBERAL PARTY

FEBRUARY 8, 1677 Andrew Marvell, English poet and parliamentarian during the Anglo-Dutch wars, publishes his last known work. "There has now for divers years a design been carried on to change the lawful government of England into an absolute tyranny." —AN ACCOUNT OF THE GROWTH OF POPERY AND ARBITRARY GOVERNMENT IN ENGLAND

FEBRUARY 8, 1996 John Perry Barlow publishes "A Declaration of the Independence of Cyberspace" in response to an anti-pornography bill passed by the US Congress that would have chilled online speech dramatically. "On behalf of the future, I ask you of the past to leave us alone."

FEBRUARY 10, 1883 The Russian revolutionary Vera Figner is arrested for her role in Tsar Alexander II's assassination. She received a death sentence that was later commuted. "My past experience had convinced me that the only way to change the existing order was by force." —MEMOIRS OF A REVOLUTIONIST

FEBRUARY 11, 1916 Emma Goldman, anarchist agitator, publisher and all-around "rebel woman," is arrested for distributing a pamphlet about birth control written by Margaret Sanger.

FEBRUARY 11, 1990 Nelson Mandela is freed after twenty-seven years as a political prisoner. Four years later he became the first president of post-apartheid South Africa.

WEDNESDAY FEBRUARY 9

Vera Nikolayevna Figner (1852–1942) after the 1905 Russian Revolution

THURSDAY FEBRUARY 10

NOTES:

FRIDAY FEBRUARY 11

SATURDAY FEBRUARY 12

SUNDAY FEBRUARY 13

_____

_____

_____

_____

_____

_____

_____

_____

MONDAY FEBRUARY 14

_____

_____

_____

_____

_____

_____

_____

TUESDAY FEBRUARY 15

_____

_____

_____

_____

_____

_____

_____

FEBRUARY 14, 1818 The birth date chosen by Frederick Douglass, America's foremost abolitionist writer and activist. "What, to the American slave, is your 4th of July? I answer: a day that reveals to him, more than all other days in the year, the gross injustice and cruelty to which he is the constant victim." —"THE MEANING OF JULY FOURTH FOR THE NEGRO"

FEBRUARY 15, 1855 Muktabai, a fourteen-year-old Dalit, publishes the earliest surviving piece of writing by an "untouchable" woman. "Let that religion, where only one person is privileged and the rest are deprived, perish from the earth and let it never enter our minds to be proud of such a religion." —"ABOUT THE GRIEFS OF THE MANGS AND MAHARS"

FEBRUARY 17, 1958 The Campaign for Nuclear Disarmament is founded in Britain; it would become the country's most important protest movement during the late 1950s and early 1960s.

FEBRUARY 18, 1934 Black lesbian poet Audre Lorde is born in New York City.

"For all of us
this instant and this triumph
We were never meant to survive."
—"A LITANY FOR SURVIVAL"

FEBRUARY 19, 1942 Japanese American internment begins in the US through Executive Order 9066.

FEBRUARY 19, 1963 Betty Friedan's _The Feminine Mystique_, a classic of second-wave feminism, is published. "The problem lay buried, unspoken, for many years in the minds of American women."

WEDNESDAY FEBRUARY 16

_____
_____
_____
_____
_____
_____
_____

Audre Lorde © Robert Alexander, 1983

THURSDAY FEBRUARY 17

_____
_____
_____
_____
_____
_____
_____

NOTES:

_____
_____
_____
_____
_____
_____

FRIDAY FEBRUARY 18

_____
_____
_____
_____
_____
_____

SATURDAY FEBRUARY 19

_____
_____
_____
_____
_____
_____

THE LUDDITES ARE RIGHT
ABOUT WHY YOU HATE YOUR JOB
GAVIN MUELLER

In light of a history rife with workers destroying machines, why do the Luddites cast the longest shadow? It is not only because they knew how to spin a good yarn. After all, the Crown doesn't muster a military force of thousands to destroy a myth. The Luddites loom large because of the power of their struggle, both in literature and in their historical accomplishments. While E.P. Thompson has sought to rescue the Luddites from "the enormous condescension of posterity" through an act of radical sympathy, he still acknowledged that militant reactions against industrialism "may have been foolhardy. But they lived through these times of acute social disturbance, and we did not." I admire Thompson's ability to comprehend the Luddites from within their specific conjuncture, rather than from a point of view that sees them as a mere speed bump on the road to our inevitable present.

But we can go further. History has a shape, but it is not one that is foretold, still less one forecast by the tools and technologies at hand. Instead, the shape of history, as Marx argued, is wrought by the struggles of those who participated in it. That the Luddites were ultimately unsuccessful is not itself an indictment: final success is a poor criterion for judging an action before or during the fact. And, as I hope to demonstrate, Luddism was not altogether pointless. Our history is the Luddites' as well, and their insight—that technology was political, and that it could and, in many cases, should be opposed—has carried down through all manner of militant movements, including those of the present. There is much to learn from this tradition, even among the most technophilic current-day radicals.

The Luddite opposition to machines was, it must be said, not a simple technophobia. As Kirkpatrick Sale, author of *Rebels Against the Future: The Luddites and Their War on the Industrial Revolution*, notes, many of the Luddites were weavers or other skilled textile workers who operated their own complicated tools. Their revolt was not against machines in themselves, but against the industrial society that threatened their established ways of life, and of which machines were the chief weapon. To say they fought machines makes about as much sense as saying a boxer fights against fists. As Sale describes it, the Luddite rebellions were never simply against technology, but "what that machinery stood for: the palpable, daily evidence of their having to succumb to forces beyond their control."

Machine breaking was only one technique among many that the Luddites deployed, reserved for use against the most intransigent factory owners as part of a wider strategy to increase worker power. Weavers invoked King Ludd in their attempts to collectively bargain for piece rates that would allow them to survive, and in their petitions to government authorities for redress. One letter sent to the Home Office in 1812, signed "Ned Lud's Office, Sherwood Forest," stated that "all frames of whatsoever discription the worckmen of which Are not paid in the current Coin of the realm will Invarioably be distroy'd," while vowing to protect the frames of compliant owners.

In historian Eric Hobsbawm's estimation, the working-class activity of the Luddites has to be understood in terms of its existing technical composition; indeed, workers had not yet been organized into a disciplined mass but were instead a mélange of laborers working in their own homes and shops, often with their own tools. Physically separated and without established organizations, they often related to bosses according to individualized contracts, and so it was impossible for them to engage in the kinds of militancy we associate with trade unions made up of mass workers. But Hobsbawm suggests something further: that through machine breaking itself, the Luddites composed themselves as a class by creating bonds of solidarity.

This is a revised extract from Breaking Things at Work: The Luddites Are Right About Why You Hate Your Job *by Gavin Mueller (Verso, 2021).*

SUNDAY FEBRUARY 20

_____

_____

_____

_____

_____

_____

_____

MONDAY FEBRUARY 21

_____

_____

_____

_____

_____

_____

_____

TUESDAY FEBRUARY 22

_____

_____

_____

_____

_____

_____

FEBRUARY 21, 1848 The _Communist Manifesto_, written by Friedrich Engels and Karl Marx, is published. "The proletarians have nothing to lose but their chains. They have a world to win."

FEBRUARY 21, 1965 Malcolm X is assassinated at the Audubon Ballroom in New York City. "Uncle Sam's hands are dripping with blood, dripping with the blood of the black man in this country." —"THE BALLOT OR THE BULLET"

FEBRUARY 23, 1848 French revolutionaries overthrow the Orléans monarchy and establish the Second Republic, where socialist Louis Blanc attempts to implement worker cooperatives. "What does competition mean to working men? It is the distribution of work to the highest bidder." —"THE ORGANIZATION OF LABOUR"

FEBRUARY 23, 1934 George Padmore, leading Pan-Africanist born in Trinidad, is expelled from the Comintern and shifts his focus to African independence struggles. "The black man certainly has to pay dear for carrying the white man's burden." —"THE WHITE MAN'S BURDEN"

FEBRUARY 24, 1895 Cuba's final War of Independence from Spain begins, planned in part by poet and revolutionary philosopher José Martí. "A cloud of ideas is a thing no armored prow can smash through." —"OUR AMERICA"

FEBRUARY 26, 1906 Upton Sinclair's exposé on the meat packing industry, _The Jungle_, is published, prompting the enactment of the Meat Inspection and Pure Food and Drug Acts.

WEDNESDAY FEBRUARY 23

Malcolm X (1925-1965) by Ed Ford, World Telegram staff photographer

THURSDAY FEBRUARY 24

NOTES:

FRIDAY FEBRUARY 25

SATURDAY FEBRUARY 26

SUNDAY FEBRUARY 27

_____

_____

_____

_____

_____

_____

_____

MONDAY FEBRUARY 28

_____

_____

_____

_____

_____

_____

_____

TUESDAY MARCH 1

_____

_____

_____

_____

_____

_____

_____

FEBRUARY 27, 1832 Auguste Blanqui, French revolutionary and early theorist of class struggle, is found guilty (with fourteen others) of supporting republicanism. "This is the war between the rich and the poor: the rich wanted it so, for they are the aggressors. But they find it wrong that the poor fight back." —BLANQUI'S DEFENSE SPEECH

FEBRUARY 27, 1973 Oglala Lakota and American Indian Movement members, including Leonard Peltier, begin an occupation of Wounded Knee, South Dakota on the Pine Ridge Indian Reservation.

MARCH 1, 1896 Ethiopian fighters defeat Italian forces at the Battle of Adwa, securing Ethiopian sovereignty to become a symbol of African resistance against European colonialism. "Once a white snake has bitten you, you will find no cure for it." —ETHIOPIAN REBEL LEADER BAHTA HAGOS

MARCH 1, 1940 Richard Wright's seminal novel _Native Son_, about a black youth living on Chicago's South Side, is published. His writings would shift the US discourse on race.

> "FB eye under my bed
> Told me all I dreamed last night, every word
> I said."
>   —"FB EYE BLUES"

MARCH 1, 1954 Lolita Lebrón and comrades open fire on the US House of Representatives in the struggle for Puerto Rican independence. "I did not come to kill anyone, I came to die for Puerto Rico." —LEBRÓN, WORDS UPON ARREST

MARCH 2, 1444 Albanian resistance leader Skanderbeg founds the League of Lezhë, uniting Balkan chieftains to fight the invading Ottoman army.

WEDNESDAY MARCH 2

_____

_____

_____

_____

_____

_____

_____

Lolita Lebrón (1919–2010) following her arrest in 1954

THURSDAY MARCH 3

_____

_____

_____

_____

_____

_____

_____

NOTES:

_____

_____

_____

_____

_____

_____

FRIDAY MARCH 4

_____

_____

_____

_____

_____

_____

SATURDAY MARCH 5

_____

_____

_____

_____

_____

SUNDAY MARCH 6

_____

_____

_____

_____

_____

_____

_____

MONDAY MARCH 7

_____

_____

_____

_____

_____

_____

_____

TUESDAY MARCH 8

_____

_____

_____

_____

_____

_____

_____

MARCH 6, 1923 The Egyptian Feminist Union is established. "They rise in times of trouble when the wills of men are tried." —ACTIVIST HUDA SHAARAWI, *HAREM YEARS: THE MEMOIRS OF AN EGYPTIAN FEMINIST, 1879–1924*

MARCH 6, 1957 The leader of the Gold Coast's imperialism fight against the British, Pan-Africanist Kwame Nkrumah, becomes the first prime minister of independent Ghana.

MARCH 6, 1984 Coal miners walk out at Cortonwood Colliery in South Yorkshire, beginning the yearlong UK miner's strike, the longest in history. "I'd rather be a picket than a scab." —PICKET LINE SLOGAN

MARCH 7, 1921 At the Kronstadt naval base, Russia's Red Army attacks sailors, soldiers and civilians who are protesting widespread famine and the Bolshevik repression of strikes. "This unrest shows clearly enough that the party has lost the faith of the working masses." —PETROPAVLOVSK RESOLUTION AND DEMANDS

MARCH 7, 1942 Lucy Parsons, anarchist and Industrial Workers of the World cofounder who was born in slavery, dies in Chicago. "Stroll you down the avenues of the rich and look through the magnificent plate windows into their voluptuous homes, and here you will discover the *very identical robbers* who have despoiled you and yours." —"TO TRAMPS"

MARCH 8, 1914 First International Women's Day, cofounded by German Marxist Clara Zetkin, is established on this day of the year. "What made women's labour particularly attractive to the capitalists was not only its lower price but also the greater submissiveness of women."

WEDNESDAY MARCH 9

_____

_____

_____

_____

_____

_____

_____

Lucy Parsons (1853–1942) after her arrest for rioting at a 1915
unemployment protest

THURSDAY MARCH 10

_____

_____

_____

_____

_____

_____

_____

NOTES:

_____

_____

_____

_____

_____

_____

FRIDAY MARCH 11

_____

_____

_____

_____

_____

_____

SATURDAY MARCH 12

_____

_____

_____

_____

_____

_____

SUNDAY MARCH 13

_____

_____

_____

_____

_____

_____

_____

MONDAY MARCH 14

_____

_____

_____

TUESDAY MARCH 15

_____

_____

_____

_____

_____

_____

_____

MARCH 13, 1933 The poet Abdukhaliq Uyghur is executed by the Chinese government for encouraging rebellion and supporting Uyghur independence.

MARCH 13, 1979 Maurice Bishop's New Jewel Movement overthrows the Grenada government, the first armed socialist revolution in a predominantly black country outside of Africa. "The true meaning of revolutionary democracy ... is a growth in fraternal love."

MARCH 14, 2008 Riots break out in Lhasa and spread throughout Tibet, targeting Han Chinese residents and businesses. "The oppressors' snipers are still standing above Tibetan people's heads; on sunny days, the beams deflected from the guns in their hands stab into the prostrating Tibetans. This is a collective memory which has been engraved on Tibetan people's hearts."
—TIBETAN POET WOESER

MARCH 15, 1845 Friedrich Engels publishes _The Condition of the Working Class in England._

MARCH 15, 1960 A student demonstration against the fraudulent election victory of South Korean strongman Syngman Rhee was attacked by police. One month later, the body of student protester Kim Ju-yul washed ashore, his skull split open by a tear-gas grenade. The public outrage would eventually result in the April Revolution, which would end Rhee's rule.

MARCH 18, 1834 Six farm workers from Tolpuddle, England, are sentenced to penal transportation to Australia for forming a trade union. "Labour is the poor man's property, from which all protection is withheld. Has not then the working man as much right to preserve and protect his labour as the rich man has his capital?" —TOLPUDDLE MARTYR GEORGE LOVELESS, _THE VICTIMS OF WHIGGERY_

WEDNESDAY MARCH 16

Paris Commune: a barricade on Rue Voltaire, after its capture by the regular army during the Bloody Week

THURSDAY MARCH 17

NOTES:

FRIDAY MARCH 18

SATURDAY MARCH 19

SUNDAY MARCH 20

_____

_____

_____

_____

_____

_____

_____

MONDAY MARCH 21

_____

_____

_____

_____

_____

_____

_____

TUESDAY MARCH 22

_____

_____

_____

_____

_____

_____

MARCH 21, 1960 South African police kill sixty-nine protesters in the Sharpeville Massacre, forcing the anti-apartheid movement underground.

MARCH 23, 1918 Avant-garde artist Tristan Tzara issues the Dada Manifesto, a politico-artistic movement whose anti-bourgeois stance would influence the Situationists and the Beats. "DADA DADA DADA—the roar of contorted pains, the interweaving of contraries and all contradictions, freaks and irrelevancies: LIFE."

MARCH 23, 1931 Revolutionary Bhagat Singh, who threw a bomb into India's central legislative assembly, is hanged by the British Raj. "Let me tell you, British rule is here not because God wills it but because they possess power and we do not dare to oppose them." —"WHY AM I AN ATHEIST?"

MARCH 24, 1977 Argentine journalist Rodolfo Walsh publishes his "Open Letter from a Writer to the Military Junta," accusing them of disappearing thousands of Argentines. The next day he is murdered. "They are the victims of a doctrine of collective guilt, which long ago disappeared from the norms of justice of any civilized community."

MARCH 24, 1980 Oscar Romero, archbishop of San Salvador in El Salvador and critic of the Salvadorean death squads, is assassinated while giving mass. "We are your people. The peasants you kill are your own brothers and sisters."

MARCH 24, 1987 First demonstration of ACT UP, pioneering direct-action AIDS organization, on Wall Street to protest Food and Drug Administration inaction on drug development. "Silence = Death" —ACT UP LOGO

WEDNESDAY MARCH 23

The iconic poster of ACT UP, 1987

THURSDAY MARCH 24

NOTES:

FRIDAY MARCH 25

SATURDAY MARCH 26

CAPITALISM CANNOT BE REFORMED  AND THE EARTH CANNOT BE REPLACED

✧ DYLANMINER.COM

Capitalism Cannot Be Reformed by Dylan A.T. Miner
(Justseeds Artists' Cooperative/justseeds.org)

Sustainable Growth by Meredith Stern
(Justseeds Artists' Cooperative/justseeds.org)

SUNDAY MARCH 27

_____

_____

_____

_____

_____

_____

_____

MONDAY MARCH 28

_____

_____

_____

_____

_____

_____

_____

TUESDAY MARCH 29

_____

_____

_____

_____

_____

_____

_____

MARCH 27, 1969 First national Chicano Youth Conference is hosted in Denver by Crusade for Justice, the civil rights organization founded by former boxer Corky Gonzáles.

> "I have come a long way to nowhere,
> unwillingly dragged by that
> monstrous, technical,
> industrial giant
> called
> Progress
> and Anglo success ..."
> —GONZÁLES, "I AM JOAQUIN"

MARCH 29, 1942 The Hukbalahap (Philippine communist guerrilla organization) is founded; its insurgency against the government lasts eight years. "Our friends in Manila refer to us as being 'outside.' That is incorrect terminology ... We are on the inside of the struggle." —PEASANT LEADER LUIS TARUC, _BORN OF THE PEOPLE_

MARCH 30, 1892 Freethinker Robert Ingersoll, favorite orator of Walt Whitman, delivers a eulogy for the poet after his death. "Whoever produces anything by weary labor, does not need a revelation from heaven to teach him that he has a right to the thing produced." —INGERSOLL, "SOME MISTAKES OF MOSES"

APRIL 1, 1649 Poor farmers begin digging plots at Saint George's Hill in Surrey, in one of the first acts of the Digger movement that sought to abolish property and wages, in some instances by occupying common land. "We are resolved to be cheated no longer, nor be held under the slavish fear of you no longer, seeing the Earth was made for us, as well as for you." —MOVEMENT FOUNDER GERRARD WINSTANLEY, "DECLARATION FROM THE POOR OPPRESSED PEOPLE OF ENGLAND"

WEDNESDAY MARCH 30

Rodolfo "Corky" Gonzáles, Mexican American boxer, poet, and political activist

THURSDAY MARCH 31

NOTES:

FRIDAY APRIL 1

SATURDAY APRIL 2

APRIL 3, 1874 Wong Chin Foo, publisher of the first Chinese American newspaper, is naturalized as a US citizen. "The difference between the heathen and the Christian is that the heathen does good for the sake of doing good."

APRIL 3, 1895 Playwright and essayist Oscar Wilde goes on trial for homosexual activity and is imprisoned for two years. "It is immoral to use private property in order to alleviate the horrible evils that result from the institution of private property." —"THE SOUL OF MAN UNDER SOCIALISM"

APRIL 4, 1968 Martin Luther King, Jr. is assassinated. "A true revolution of values will soon look uneasily on the glaring contrast of poverty and wealth." —"BEYOND VIETNAM: A TIME TO BREAK SILENCE"

APRIL 5, 1971 The "Manifesto of the 343," signed by 343 women (including Simone de Beauvoir) who had had secret abortions, demands that the French government legalize the procedure.

APRIL 5, 1976 On the traditional day of mourning, thousands of Beijingers lay wreaths and poems on Tiananmen Square, indirectly criticizing the Cultural Revolution.

"If a thousand challengers lie beneath your feet, Count me as number thousand and one."
—BEI DAO, "THE ANSWER," WHICH BECAME AN ANTHEM OF THE DEMOCRACY MOVEMENT

APRIL 8, 1950 Imprisoned for sedition, the revolutionary Turkish poet Nazim Hikmet launches a hunger strike for amnesty for political prisoners.

"Galloping from farthest Asia
and jutting into the Mediterranean
like a mare's head
this country is ours."
—"INVITATION"

WEDNESDAY APRIL 6

_____
_____
_____
_____
_____
_____
_____

Dr. Martin Luther King, Jr. (1929–1968) being arrested in 1956 during the Montgomery Bus Boycott

THURSDAY APRIL 7

_____
_____
_____
_____
_____
_____
_____

NOTES:

_____
_____
_____
_____
_____
_____

FRIDAY APRIL 8

_____
_____
_____
_____
_____
_____

SATURDAY APRIL 9

_____
_____
_____
_____
_____
_____

SUNDAY APRIL 10

_____

_____

_____

_____

_____

_____

_____

MONDAY APRIL 11

_____

_____

_____

_____

_____

_____

TUESDAY APRIL 12

_____

_____

_____

_____

_____

_____

APRIL 10, 1919 Emiliano Zapata, Mexican Revolution leader, is assassinated by the government. "The nation is tired of false men and traitors who make promises like liberators and who on arriving in power forget them and constitute themselves as tyrants."

APRIL 11, 1981 Riots break out in the Caribbean London neighborhood of Brixton in response to police targeting of young black men under the Sus law. The fighting lasts for three days.

APRIL 11, 2007 Kurt Vonnegut, author of novels with anti-authoritarian and anti-war themes, dies.

APRIL 13, 1635 Fakhr al-Din II, Druze independence leader against the Ottoman Empire and Lebanon's first freedom fighter, is executed. "No promise of reward or threat of punishment will dissuade us." —MESSAGE TO THE PEOPLE

APRIL 14, 1428 Vietnamese forces are victorious after a ten-year rebellion against their Chinese rulers. "Today it is a case of the grasshopper pitted against the elephant. But tomorrow the elephant will have its guts ripped out." —REBELLION LEADER LÊ LOI'S VICTORY SPEECH

APRIL 14, 2002 Venezuelan president Hugo Chávez, who described his socialist movement as the Bolivarian Revolution, returns to power after having been ousted in a US-backed coup two days earlier. "What we now have to do is define the future of the world. Dawn is breaking out all over." —ADDRESS TO THE UN GENERAL ASSEMBLY

APRIL 15, 1936 The Great Revolt begins in Palestine against British Mandate and Zionism, lasting three years. "They stepped all over us until we couldn't take any more. This went on until the rebellion was smashed." —MAHMOUD ABOU DEEB, WITNESS TO THE REVOLT

WEDNESDAY APRIL 13

_____
_____
_____
_____
_____
_____
_____

The Brixton Riots, 1981

THURSDAY APRIL 14

_____
_____
_____
_____
_____
_____
_____

NOTES:

_____
_____
_____
_____
_____
_____

FRIDAY APRIL 15

_____
_____
_____
_____
_____
_____
_____

SATURDAY APRIL 16

_____
_____
_____
_____
_____
_____
_____

SUNDAY APRIL 17

MONDAY APRIL 18

TUESDAY APRIL 19

APRIL 18, 1955 Twenty-nine newly independent African and Asian countries meet at the Bandung Conference in Indonesia, in a show of strength for the Non-Aligned Movement. "Without peace, our independence means little." —OPENING SPEECH BY INDONESIAN LEADER SUKARNO

APRIL 20, 1773 Peter Bestes and others deliver a petition for freedom "in behalf of our fellow slaves" to the Massachusetts legislature. "The divine spirit of freedom seems to fire every human breast on the continent, except such as are bribed to assist in executing the execrable plan."

APRIL 21, 1913 The Indian revolutionary group, the Ghadar Party, is formed by Punjabis in North America. "The nation-state may truly be compared to the dinosaurs and the tyrannosaurus of the Mesozoic Age. Like those gigantic reptiles, the modern nation-state has a very small brain with which to think and plan, but tremendously powerful teeth with which to tear and rend, to destroy and dismember." —FOUNDER LALA HAR DAYAL, "HINTS OF SELF-CULTURE"

APRIL 22, 1977 Kenyan activist Wangari Maathai founds the Green Belt Movement, an environmental nonprofit aimed at empowering poor, rural women. "Until you dig a hole, you plant a tree, you water it and make it survive, you haven't done a thing."

APRIL 23, 1968 Students occupy buildings in New York's Columbia University to protest the school's ties to a defense contractor, triggering a campus-wide strike. "Up against the wall, Motherfuckers!" —PROTEST GRAFFITI

WEDNESDAY APRIL 20

UC Berkeley students of the Ghadar Movement, 1915

THURSDAY APRIL 21

NOTES:

FRIDAY APRIL 22

SATURDAY APRIL 23

V

NO MORE EXCUSES FOR PASSIVITY

ANDREAS MALM

The cycles of intense climate activity have not returned to square one, but rather formed a cumulative process and rising loop, like the climate crisis itself. The American and European sections have learnt from each other—divestment coming to English campuses, Greta Thunberg sailing to New York—and the cadres have accumulated a wealth of experiences. These include "small wins"—a gas pipeline cancelled here, a coal plant scrapped there—as well as some big losses, which, however, seem to ensure the movement its growth, as the fire drives more people to take the plunge into activism. But so far, the movement has stopped short of one mode of action: offensive (or for that matter defensive) physical force. Anything that could be classified as violence has been studiously, scrupulously avoided. Indeed, the commitment to absolute non-violence appears

to have stiffened over the cycles, the internalisation of its ethos universal, the discipline remarkable.

Will absolute non-violence be the only way, forever the sole admissible tactic in the struggle to abolish fossil fuels? Can we be sure that it will suffice against this enemy? Must we tie ourselves to its mast to reach a safer place? The question can be formulated in a different way. Imagine that the mass mobilisations of the third cycle become impossible to ignore. The ruling classes feel themselves under such heat—perhaps their hearts even melting somewhat at the sight of all these kids with handwritten placards—that their obduracy wanes. New politicians are voted into office, notably from green parties in Europe, who live up to their election promises. The pressure is kept up from below. Moratoriums on fresh fossil fuel

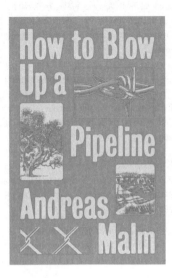

infrastructure are instituted. Germany initiates immediate phase-out of coal production, the Netherlands likewise for gas, Norway for oil, the US for all of the above; legislation and planning are put in place for cutting emissions by at least 10 per cent per year; renewable energy and public transport are scaled up, plant-based diets promoted, blanket bans on fossil fuels prepared. The movement should be given the chance to see this scenario through.

But imagine a different scenario: a few years down the road, the kids of the Thunberg generation and the rest of us wake up one morning and realise that business-as-usual is still on, regardless of all the strikes, the science, the pleas, the millions with colourful outfits and banners—not beyond the realm of the thinkable. Imagine the greasy wheels roll as fast as ever. What do we do then? Do we say that we've done what we could, tried the means at our disposal and failed? Do we conclude that the only thing left is learning to die—a position already propounded by some—and slide down the side of the crater into three, four, eight degrees of warming? Or is there another phase, beyond peaceful protest?

At what point do we escalate? When do we conclude that the time has come to also try something different? When do we start physically attacking the things that consume our planet and destroy them with our own hands? Is there a good reason we have waited this long?

This is a revised extract from How to Blow Up a Pipeline: Learning to Fight in a World on Fire *by Andreas Malm (Verso, 2021).*

SUNDAY APRIL 24

_____

_____

_____

_____

_____

_____

MONDAY APRIL 25

_____

_____

_____

_____

_____

_____

TUESDAY APRIL 26

_____

_____

_____

_____

_____

_____

_____

APRIL 24, 1916 Irish republicans mount an armed insurrection against the British imperialists on Easter week, in what became known as the Easter Rising.

APRIL 25, 1974 Portuguese armed forces overthrow the ruling Estado Novo dictatorship in what becomes known as the Carnation Revolution, setting the stage for its colonies to achieve independence.

APRIL 26, 1937 The Basque town of Guernica is destroyed in an aerial bombing by German and Italian forces, in one of the most sordid episodes of the Spanish Civil War.

"Faces good in firelight good in frost
Refusing the night the wounds and blows."
—SURREALIST POET PAUL ELUARD, "VICTORY OF
GUERNICA"

APRIL 28, 1967 Heavyweight champion boxer Muhammad Ali refuses induction into the US Armed Forces, leading to a charge for draft evasion and being stripped of his titles. "I ain't got no quarrel with them Vietcong. No Vietcong ever called me nigger."

APRIL 29, 1992 Los Angeles residents begin rioting after the four police officers accused of beating Rodney King are acquitted. "Give us the hammer and the nails, we will rebuild the city." —BLOODS AND CRIPS, "PLAN FOR THE RECONSTRUCTION OF LOS ANGELES"

WEDNESDAY APRIL 27

The Proclamation of the Irish Republic, 1916

THURSDAY APRIL 28

NOTES:

FRIDAY APRIL 29

SATURDAY APRIL 30

SUNDAY MAY 1

_____

_____

_____

_____

_____

_____

MONDAY MAY 2

_____

_____

_____

_____

_____

_____

TUESDAY MAY 3

_____

_____

_____

_____

_____

_____

MAY 1, 1949 Albert Einstein publishes "Why Socialism?" in the inaugural issue of *Monthly Review*. "The economic anarchy of capitalist society as it exists today is, in my opinion, the real source of the evil."

MAY 1, 1970 Lesbian activists deliver their manifesto at the Second Congress to Unite Women in New York City, to protest the exclusion of lesbian speakers. "Lesbian is a label invented by the man to throw at any woman who dares to be his equal." —RADICALESBIANS, "THE WOMAN-IDENTIFIED WOMAN"

MAY 4, 1886 At a rally for the eight-hour day at Haymarket Square in Chicago, a bomb is thrown at police and eight anarchists are later convicted of conspiracy. "I repeat that I am the enemy of the 'order' of today, and I repeat that, with all my powers, so long as breath remains in me, I shall combat it." —LOUIS LINGG'S TRIAL SPEECH

MAY 4, 1919 Chinese students demonstrate in Beijing, sparking the anti-Confucian New Culture Movement. "Wanting to eat men, at the same time afraid of being eaten themselves, they all eye each other with the deepest suspicion." —LU XUN, *A MADMAN'S DIARY*, ONE OF THE MOVEMENT'S REPRESENTATIVE WORKS

MAY 5, 1938 Second and final arrest of Russian poet Osip Mandelstam, for writing critically of Stalin.

"He forges decrees in a line like horseshoes
One for the groin, one the forehead, temple, eye"
—"THE STALIN EPIGRAM"

MAY 5, 1966 Jit Poumisak, Thai Marxist poet and revolutionary, is killed after retreating to the jungle with the outlawed Communist Party. "[The Thai people] have been able to identify clearly the enemies who plunder them and skin them alive and suck the very marrow from their bones." —"THE REAL FACE OF THAI SAKTINA [FEUDALISM] TODAY"

WEDNESDAY MAY 4

Attention Workingmen!

GREAT

MASS-MEETING

TO-NIGHT, at 7.30 o'clock,

AT THE

HAYMARKET, Randolph St., Bet. Desplaines and Halsted.

Good Speakers will be present to denounce the latest atrocious act of the police, the shooting of our fellow-workmen yesterday afternoon.

Workingmen Arm Yourselves and Appear in Full Force!

THE EXECUTIVE COMMITTEE.

Achtung, Arbeiter!

The first flier calling for a rally in the Haymarket on May 4, 1886

THURSDAY MAY 5

NOTES:

FRIDAY MAY 6

SATURDAY MAY 7

SUNDAY MAY 8

MONDAY MAY 9

TUESDAY MAY 10

MAY 9, 1918 Scottish revolutionary John Maclean, on trial for sedition for opposing WWI, delivers a rousing speech from the dock. "I am here as the accuser of capitalism, dripping with blood from head to foot."

MAY 11, 1930 Pedro Albizu Campos is elected president of the Puerto Rican Nationalist Party. "The empire is a system. It can wait. It can fatten its victims to render its digestion more enjoyable at a later time."

MAY 10, 1857 Rebellion against British rule in India begins, eventually growing into the First Indian War of Independence.

MAY 10, 1872 Victoria Woodhull, suffragist and publisher of the first English edition of *The Communist Manifesto*, becomes the first woman nominated for president of the US.

MAY 11, 1894 Three thousand employees of the Pullman railcar company go on strike, eventually growing to 250,000 workers before being crushed by federal troops.

MAY 12, 1916 James Connolly is tied to a chair and shot by the British government for his role in the Easter Rising—the precursor to the declaration of the Irish Republic in 1919. Born in Scotland to Irish immigrant parents, Connolly became a leader of the socialist movement in Scotland, Ireland and the United States, where he was a member of the Socialist Party and the IWW.

MAY 13, 1968 French workers join students in a one-day strike, with over a million protesters marching through Paris streets. By the following week, two-thirds of France's workforce was on strike, becoming the largest general strike that had ever stopped the economy of an industrialized country.

WEDNESDAY MAY 11

_____

_____

_____

_____

_____

_____

_____

Victoria Woodhull, suffragist and publisher of the first English edition of _The Communist Manifesto_

THURSDAY MAY 12

_____

_____

_____

_____

_____

_____

_____

NOTES:

FRIDAY MAY 13

_____

_____

_____

_____

_____

_____

SATURDAY MAY 14

_____

_____

_____

_____

_____

_____

SUNDAY MAY 15

_____

_____

_____

_____

_____

_____

_____

MONDAY MAY 16

_____

_____

_____

_____

_____

_____

_____

TUESDAY MAY 17

_____

_____

_____

_____

_____

_____

_____

MAY 16, 1943 Warsaw Ghetto Uprising, which began in German-occupied Poland to resist the last deportation of Jews to the Treblinka extermination camp, ends in failure. "We decided to gamble for our lives." —MAREK EDELMAN, MEMBER OF THE JEWISH COMBAT ORGANIZATION

MAY 17, 1649 A mutiny in the New Model Army of England by the Levellers, who called for the expansion of suffrage, religious toleration, and sweeping political reforms, is crushed when its leaders are executed. "We do now hold ourselves bound in mutual duty to each other to take the best care we can for the future to avoid both the danger of returning into a slavish condition and the chargeable remedy of another war." —LEVELLERS, "AGREEMENT OF THE PEOPLE"

MAY 18, 1980 Citizens of Kwangju, South Korea, seize control of their city, demanding democratization, an end to martial law, and an increase in the minimum wage.

MAY 19, 1869 US president Ulysses S. Grant issues the National Eight Hour Law Proclamation, an early but symbolic victory for the struggle over the working day in the US. "Think carefully of the difference between the operative and the mechanic leaving his work at half-past seven (after dark, the most of the year), and that of the more leisurely walk home at half-past four p.m., or three hours earlier." —MACHINIST-TURNED-ACTIVIST IRA STEWARD, "THE EIGHT HOUR MOVEMENT"

MAY 19, 1946 Millions of Japanese take part in the Food May Day demonstrations, protesting the country's broken food delivery system.

WEDNESDAY MAY 18

_____

_____

_____

_____

_____

_____

_____

Children participating in the protest known as Food May Day for
food supplies in Japan, 1946

THURSDAY MAY 19

_____

_____

_____

_____

_____

_____

_____

NOTES:

_____

_____

_____

_____

_____

_____

FRIDAY MAY 20

_____

_____

_____

_____

_____

_____

_____

SATURDAY MAY 21

_____

_____

_____

_____

_____

_____

_____

SUNDAY MAY 22

_____

_____

_____

_____

_____

_____

MONDAY MAY 23

_____

_____

_____

_____

_____

_____

_____

TUESDAY MAY 24

_____

_____

_____

_____

_____

_____

_____

MAY 24, 1798 Society of United Irishmen, a republican group influenced by the American and French revolutions, rises up against English rule in what becomes the Irish Rebellion.

"A wet winter, a dry spring
A bloody summer, and no King."
—IRISH SAYING

MAY 25, 1899 Bengal's "rebel poet" Kazi Nazrul Islam is born.

"And I shall rest, battle-weary rebel, only on the day
when the wails of the oppressed shall not rend the air and sky."
—"THE REBEL"

MAY 28, 1913 Six hundred black women march through Bloemfontein, South Africa to protest the law requiring them, as non-white workers, to carry proof of employment.

"Too long have they submitted
to white malignity;
No passes they would carry
but assert their dignity."
—POEM INSPIRED BY THE EVENT, SIGNED "JOHNNY THE OFFICE BOY"

MAY 28, 1918 First Republic of Armenia is declared, following the Armenian Resistance of 1914–18.

MAY 28, 1892 The Sierra Club, which sought to conserve nature and establish national parks, is founded by Scottish-born American John Muir. "Our magnificent redwoods and much of the sugar-pine forests of Sierra Nevada [have] been absorbed by foreign and resident capitalists." —"THE DESTRUCTION OF THE REDWOODS"

WEDNESDAY MAY 25

_____

_____

_____

_____

_____

_____

_____

Armenian Revolutionary Federation fighters, banner reading
"Liberty or Death"

THURSDAY MAY 26

_____

_____

_____

_____

_____

_____

_____

NOTES:

_____

_____

_____

_____

_____

_____

FRIDAY MAY 27

_____

_____

_____

_____

_____

_____

_____

SATURDAY MAY 28

_____

_____

_____

_____

_____

_____

V

ON CONSENT
KATHERINE ANGEL

In an interview in 2020, Donna Rotunno, the lawyer defending Harvey Weinstein in trial, said that "women need to be very clear about their intentions," and "prepared for the circumstances they put themselves in." Likewise, the consent discourse urges women to know their desires ahead of sex, to "know what you want and what your partner wants." How useful is this injunction to self-knowledge? Who exactly does it serve? That both Weinstein's lawyer and consent advocates urge self-knowledge on us should give us pause.

"A woman faced with sexual advances from her date," wrote legal scholar Nicholas J. Little in a 2005 article making the case for affirmative consent, "will either want sexual intercourse or not want sexual intercourse." But a woman, a woman like Girl X or Grace, or like you or me perhaps, might not either want or not want sex; she might be hovering between these stark stances. We don't always begin with desire; it is not always there to be known. The rubric of consent is yet again not sufficient

for thinking about sex, because it glosses over something crucial to acknowledge: that we don't always know what we want.

When did we buy the idea that we know what we want, whether in sex or elsewhere? The rhetoric of consent too often implies that desire is something that lies in wait, fully formed within us, ready for us to extract. Yet our desires emerge in interaction; we don't always know what we want; sometimes we discover things we didn't know we wanted; sometimes we discover what we want only in the doing. This—that we don't always know and can't always say what we want—must be folded into the ethics of sex rather than swept aside as an inconvenience.

Another key reason, then, that consent cannot bear the weight we place on it is that it insists on an unrealizable condition for women's pleasure and safety. Desire is uncertain and unfolding, and this is unsettling. It is unsettling because it opens up the possibility of women not knowing themselves fully, and of men capitalizing on that lack of certainty by coercing or bullying them. Should we then deny this aspect of desire as a consequence? No. We must not insist on a sexual desire that is fixed and known in advance, in order to be safe. That would be to hold sexuality hostage to violence.

We don't always know what we want and we are not always able to express our desires clearly. This is in part due to the violence, misogyny and shame that make desire's discovery difficult, and its expression fraught. But it is also in the nature of desire to be social, emergent and responsive—to context, to our histories and to the desires and behaviours of others. We are social creatures; and our desires have always emerged, from day one, in relation to those who care, or do not care, for us. Desire never exists in isolation. This is also what makes sex potentially exciting, rich and meaningful. How do we make this fact galvanizing rather than paralysing?

Commentators on the "new" landscape of sex and consent often plaintively ask why it is that men are expected to be able to "read a woman's mind" when it comes to sex. My question is different: why are women asked to know their own minds, when knowing one's own mind is such an undependable aim? Self-knowledge is not a reliable feature of female sexuality, nor of sexuality in general; in fact, it is not a reliable feature of being a person. Insisting otherwise is fatal, and it's an assumption that has been conceded for far too long, to the impediment of conversations about pleasure, joy, autonomy and safety. If we want sex to be good again—or at all—anytime soon, we need

to reject this insistence, and start elsewhere. Instead of fiddling with formulations of consent on which we place too high an ethical burden, and instead of decrying women's attempts to make their worlds safer and more interested in their pleasure, we need to articulate an ethics of sex that does not try frantically to keep desire's uncertainty at bay. A sexual ethics that is worth its name has to allow for obscurity, for opacity and for not-knowing. We need to start from this very premise—this risky, complex premise: that we shouldn't have to know ourselves in order to be safe from violence.

This is an edited excerpt from Tomorrow Sex Will Be Good Again: Women and Desire in the Age of Consent *by Katherine Angel (Verso, 2021).*

TOMORROW SEX WILL BE GOOD AGAIN

WOMEN AND DESIRE IN THE AGE OF CONSENT

KATHERINE ANGEL

SUNDAY MAY 29

_____

_____

_____

_____

_____

_____

_____

MONDAY MAY 30

_____

_____

_____

_____

_____

_____

_____

TUESDAY MAY 31

_____

_____

_____

_____

_____

_____

_____

MAY 29, 1851 Sojourner Truth, abolitionist speaker, delivers her famous "Ain't I a Woman" speech to the Women's Convention in Akron, Ohio. "I can't read, but I can hear. I have heard the Bible and I learned that Eve caused man to sin. Well, if woman upset the world, do give her a chance to set it right again."

MAY 29, 1963 Peruvian revolutionary Hugo Blanco is captured after leading a "Land or Death" peasant uprising that sparked the country's first agrarian reform. Blanco was spared from execution thanks to pleas from Bertrand Russell, Jean-Paul Sartre, Simone de Beauvoir, Che Guevara, and others. "To be a revolutionary is to love the world, to love life, to be happy." —"TO MY PEOPLE," WRITTEN FROM EL FRONTÓN PENAL COLONY

JUNE 4, 1450 Jack Cade, who led 5,000 peasants through London, capturing and beheading King Henry VI's associates, issues a manifesto of grievances.

JUNE 4, 1920 The republican-socialist Jangal movement forms the short-lived Persian Soviet Socialist State in the Gilan province of Iran. "By the will of the working people, Soviet power has been organized in Persia." —LETTER TO TROTSKY FROM THE REVOLUTIONARY WAR COUNCIL OF THE PERSIAN RED ARMY

JUNE 4, 1989 As army tanks roll into Beijing's Tiananmen Square, protestors join Hou Dejian in singing his popular song, "Heirs of the Dragon."

"Enemies on all sides, the sword of the dictator.
For how many years did those gunshots resound?"

WEDNESDAY JUNE 1

Lord Saye and Sele Brought Before Jake Cade 4th July 1450
by Charles Lucy

THURSDAY JUNE 2

NOTES:

FRIDAY JUNE 3

SATURDAY JUNE 4

SUNDAY JUNE 5

_____

_____

_____

_____

_____

_____

_____

_____

MONDAY JUNE 6

_____

_____

_____

_____

_____

_____

_____

TUESDAY JUNE 7

_____

_____

_____

_____

_____

_____

_____

JUNE 5, 1940 Novelist and Yorkshire radical J. B. Priestley broadcasts his first "Postscript" radio series for the BBC, which drew audiences of up to 16 million listeners, and was soon cancelled for being too leftist. "Britain, which in the years immediately before this war was rapidly losing such democratic virtues as it possessed, is now being bombed and burned into democracy."

JUNE 5, 2013 The _Guardian_ publishes the first batch of government documents leaked by National Security Agency whistle-blower Edward Snowden.

JUNE 7, 1903 James Connolly founds the Socialist Labour Party with comrades in Edinburgh; he is later executed for his role in the Easter Uprising. "Before a shot has been fired by the British army on land, before a battle has been fought at sea, ruin and misery are entering the homes of the working people." —"WAR—WHAT IT MEANS TO YOU"

JUNE 10, 1952 Trinidadian historian, novelist and critic C.L.R. James is detained at Ellis Island to await deportation from the US. "The African bruises and breaks himself against his bars in the interests of freedoms wider than his own." —A HISTORY OF NEGRO REVOLT

JUNE 10, 1967 The June 1967 War between Israel and Syria, Jordan, and Egypt ends in Arab defeat.

"My grieved country,
In a flash
You changed me from a poet who wrote love poems
To a poet who writes with a knife."
—SYRIAN POET AND DIPLOMAT NIZAR QABBANI,
"FOOTNOTE TO THE BOOK OF SETBACK"

WEDNESDAY JUNE 8

Trinidadian historian, novelist and critic C.L.R. James

THURSDAY JUNE 9

FRIDAY JUNE 10

SATURDAY JUNE 11

SUNDAY JUNE 12

MONDAY JUNE 13

TUESDAY JUNE 14

JUNE 12, 1917 Founding of the Liberty League, the first organization of the "New Negro Movement" by Hubert Harrison, a black intellectual and labor leader who immigrated to the US from the US Virgin Islands.

JUNE 13, 1971 The *New York Times* publishes the first of the Daniel Ellsberg–leaked Pentagon Papers, which proved that the US government misled the public on the Vietnam War. "If the war was unjust, as I now regarded it, that meant that every Vietnamese killed by Americans or by the proxies we had financed since the 1950s had been killed by us without justification." —SECRETS: A MEMOIR OF VIETNAM AND THE PENTAGON PAPERS

JUNE 15, 1813 Simón Bolívar issues his "Decree of War to the Death" for independence from Spain in Trujillo, Venezuela. "Spaniards and Canarians, count on death, even if indifferent, if you do not actively work in favor of the independence of America. Americans, count on life, even if guilty."

JUNE 16, 1948 The military arm of the Malayan Communist Party fires the first shots of an insurrection against British rule. "Imperialism wants to suppress our struggle for better living conditions with guns and knives and we must answer with more vigorous and larger-scale unified struggle." —EDITORIAL IN PARTY NEWSPAPER MIN SHENG PAO

JUNE 16, 1971 The Polynesian Panther Party is formed in Auckland as a Maori and Pacific Islander civil rights group.

JUNE 18, 1984 British police attack picketing miners with dogs, riot gear and armored vehicles, in a pivotal event of the 1984–85 UK Miners' Strike.

WEDNESDAY JUNE 15

meet the representatives
of the
**POLYNESIAN
PANTHER
PARTY**
norman tuiasau
will ilolahia

Polynesian Panther Party poster, c. 1973

THURSDAY JUNE 16

NOTES:

FRIDAY JUNE 17

SATURDAY JUNE 18

SUNDAY JUNE 19

_____

_____

_____

_____

_____

_____

_____

MONDAY JUNE 20

_____

_____

_____

_____

_____

_____

_____

TUESDAY JUNE 21

_____

_____

_____

_____

_____

_____

_____

JUNE 22, 1955 Historian Eric Williams founds the People's National Movement, which later ushers in independence in Trinidad and Tobago. "The history of our West Indian islands can be expressed in two simple words: Columbus and Sugar." —CAPITALISM AND SLAVERY

JUNE 22, 1897 Indian anticolonialists shoot two British officers, and independence leader Bal Gangadhar Tilak is arrested for incitement. "Swaraj [self-rule] is my birthright and I shall have it!"

JUNE 25, 1876 Battle of Little Bighorn begins in what is now Montana, with combined Lakota, Cheyenne, and Arapaho forces beating the US 7th Cavalry. "I have robbed, killed, and injured too many white men to believe in a good peace. They are medicine, and I would eventually die a lingering death. I would rather die on the field of battle." —NATIVE LEADER SITTING BULL

JUNE 25, 1892 Ida B. Wells, civil rights activist and anti-lynching campaigner, publishes an early version of her pamphlet "Southern Horrors: Lynch Law in All Its Phases." "When the white man who is always the aggressor knows he runs as great a risk of biting the dust every time his Afro-American victim does, he will have greater respect for Afro-American life."

JUNE 25, 1962 Mozambique's anticolonial liberation party FRELIMO is founded. In the early 1970s, its guerrilla force of 7,000 fought 60,000 Portuguese colonial troops.

"In our land
bullets are beginning to flower."
—JORGE REBELO, POET BEHIND FRELIMO'S
PROPAGANDA CAMPAIGN

WEDNESDAY JUNE 22

Civil rights activst and suffragist Ida B. Wells (1862-1931)

THURSDAY JUNE 23

NOTES:

FRIDAY JUNE 24

SATURDAY JUNE 25

COVID Dreamscape by Roger Peet
(Justseeds Artists' Cooperative/justseeds.org)

Pandemic as Portal by Kill Joy
(Justseeds Artists' Cooperative/justseeds.org)

SUNDAY JUNE 26

_____

_____

_____

_____

_____

_____

_____

MONDAY JUNE 27

_____

_____

_____

_____

_____

_____

_____

TUESDAY JUNE 28

_____

_____

_____

_____

_____

_____

_____

JUNE 27, 1905 The Industrial Workers of the World is founded in Chicago, combining Marxist and trade unionist principles. "I believe we can agree that we should unite into one great organization—big enough to take in the children that are now working; big enough to take in the black man; big enough to take in all nationalities ..." —WILLIAM "BIG BILL" HAYWOOD, "THE GENERAL STRIKE"

JUNE 27, 1880 Helen Keller, world-renowned deafblind author and speaker, is born in Alabama. "If I ever contribute to the Socialist movement the book that I sometimes dream of, I know what I shall name it: Industrial Blindness and Social Deafness." —"HOW I BECAME A SOCIALIST"

JUNE 28, 1969 Riots begin at New York City's Stonewall Inn in response to a police raid, sparking the modern gay rights movement.

JUNE 30, 1840 Pierre-Joseph Proudhon, French revolutionary and first self-declared anarchist, publishes his *What Is Property?* "Property is theft!"

JUNE 30, 1855 The Santhal Rebellion, led by two brothers, sees peasants across the Bengal Presidency rise up against the British Raj and local landlords.

JULY 2, 1809 Shawnee chief Tecumseh calls on all Indians to unite against the encroachment of white settlers on native land. "The only way to stop this evil is for all the red men to unite in claiming an equal right in the land. That is how it was at first, and should be still, for the land never was divided, but was for the use of everyone." —ADDRESS TO WILLIAM HENRY HARRISON

WEDNESDAY JUNE 29

_____

_____

_____

_____

_____

_____

_____

Marsha P. Johnson and Sylvia Rivera, prominent activists who led the Stonewall Riots

THURSDAY JUNE 30

_____

_____

_____

_____

_____

_____

_____

NOTES:

_____

_____

_____

_____

_____

_____

FRIDAY JULY 1

_____

_____

_____

_____

_____

_____

_____

SATURDAY JULY 2

_____

_____

_____

_____

_____

_____

SUNDAY JULY 3

_____

_____

_____

_____

_____

_____

_____

MONDAY JULY 4

_____

_____

_____

_____

_____

_____

_____

TUESDAY JULY 5

_____

_____

_____

_____

_____

_____

_____

JULY 4, 1789 The Marquis de Sade is moved from the Bastille prison to Charenton, days before French revolutionaries storm it and set fire to his writings there. "No act of possession can ever be perpetrated on a free being; it is as unjust to own a wife monogamously as it is to own slaves." —"PHILOSOPHY IN THE BEDROOM"

JULY 4, 1876 Susan B. Anthony and other protesters present the "Declaration of Rights for Women" at an official celebration of the centennial of the United States. "Women's wealth, thought, and labor have cemented the stones of every monument man has reared to liberty."

JULY 4, 1967 The British Parliament decriminalizes homosexuality.

JULY 5, 1885 The Protect the King movement in Vietnam begins, following a French attack on the imperial capital of Hue, and uniting the country against French colonial rule. "Better to be sentenced once than sentenced for eternity." —COORDINATOR OF RESISTANCE IN NORTHERN VIETNAM NGUYỄN QUANG BÍCH, LETTER TO THE FRENCH

JULY 7, 1969 Redstockings, a New York–based radical Marxist-feminist group, publishes its manifesto. "Liberated women—very different from women's liberation!" —REDSTOCKINGS MEMBER PAT MAINARDI, "THE POLITICS OF HOUSEWORK"

JULY 9, 1910 Govan Mbeki, leader of the South African Communist Party and the African National Congress, born. Following the Rivonia Trial, Mbeki served a long-term on Robben Island, during which he managed to run education classes with prisoners, many on Marxist theory, and wrote a number of significant analyses jail.

WEDNESDAY JULY 6

Activists and supporters march outside the Rivonia Trial, 1964

THURSDAY JULY 7

NOTES:

FRIDAY JULY 8

SATURDAY JULY 9

SUNDAY JULY 10

_____

_____

_____

_____

_____

_____

_____

MONDAY JULY 11

_____

_____

_____

_____

_____

_____

_____

TUESDAY JULY 12

_____

_____

_____

_____

_____

_____

_____

JULY 13, 1524 Thomas Müntzer, radical German theologian who became a leader in the Peasants' War of 1524 to 1525, delivers his famous "Sermon to the Princes" to Saxon nobles. "Oh, you beloved lords, how well the Lord will smash down the old pots of clay [ecclesiastical authorities] with his rod of iron."

JULY 13, 1934 Nobel Prize–winning Nigerian poet and playwright Wole Soyinka is born. Over the course of his life, Soyinka is prosecuted and jailed numerous times for his outspoken political critiques.

"Traveler you must set forth
At dawn.
I promise marvels of the holy hour."
—"DEATH IN THE DAWN"

JULY 14, 1789 An organized mob breaks into a royal armory in Paris and, newly armed, storms the Bastille, a fortress that held the monarchy's political prisoners. "This very night all the Swiss and German battalions will leave the Champ de Mars to massacre us all. One resource is left; to take arms!" —SPEECH BY JOURNALIST CAMILLE DESMOULINS THAT ROUSED THE PEOPLE THE PREVIOUS DAY

JULY 14, 1877 The Great Railroad Strike begins in West Virginia, United States, pitting thousands of railroad workers against state militias and the national guardsmen summoned to break it. "Wages and revenge." —SLOGAN

WEDNESDAY JULY 13

_____

_____

_____

_____

_____

_____

_____

Blockade of engines at Martinsburg, West Virginia, 1877

THURSDAY JULY 14

_____

_____

_____

_____

_____

_____

_____

NOTES:

_____

_____

_____

_____

_____

_____

FRIDAY JULY 15

_____

_____

_____

_____

_____

_____

_____

SATURDAY JULY 16

_____

_____

_____

_____

_____

_____

_____

SUNDAY JULY 17

_____

_____

_____

_____

_____

_____

MONDAY JULY 18

_____

_____

_____

_____

_____

_____

_____

TUESDAY JULY 19

_____

_____

_____

_____

_____

_____

JULY 18, 1936 Resistance fighter Buenaventura Durruti forms the "Durruti Column," the largest anarchist fighting force in the Spanish Civil War. "The bourgeoisie might blast and ruin its own world before it leaves the stage of history. We carry a new world here, in our hearts." —DURRUTI IN AN INTERVIEW THREE MONTHS BEFORE BEING KILLED

JULY 19, 1961 The Sandinista National Liberation Front (FSLN) is founded; in 1979 it will overthrow the Somoza dictatorship in Nicaragua. "Those of us who propose to wage a struggle to liberate our country and make freedom a reality must rescue our own traditions and put together the facts and figures we need in order to wage an ideological war against our enemy." —FSLN COFOUNDER CARLOS FONSECA, SPEECH IN HAVANA

JULY 19, 1979 Ernesto Cardenal, Liberation Theology priest and poet aligned with the Sandinistas, becomes the first minister of culture under the new revolutionary government.

> "We shall celebrate in the great squares the anniversary of the Revolution
> The God that does exist is the god of the workers."
>
> —PSALM ("SALMO") 43

JULY 20, 1925 Frantz Fanon, psychiatrist and revolutionary whose writings inspired anticolonial movements throughout the world, is born in Martinique. "HISTORY teaches us clearly that the battle against colonialism does not run straight away along the lines of nationalism." —THE WRETCHED OF THE EARTH

JULY 23, 1900 W. E. B. Du Bois attends the First Pan-African Congress in London, where he makes the statement later immortalized in his 1903 book _Souls of Black Folk_: "The problem of the twentieth century is the problem of the color-line."

WEDNESDAY JULY 20

W. E. B. Du Bois—American sociologist, historian, civil rights activist, Pan-Africanist, author and editor—in 1918

THURSDAY JULY 21

NOTES:

FRIDAY JULY 22

SATURDAY JULY 23

V

BEYOND BARBARISM: TOWARDS ECOSOCIALISM
MATHEW LAWRENCE
AND LAURIE LAYBOURN-LANGTON

In 1916, amid the wreckage of war and empire, Rosa Luxemburg saw that "bourgeois society stands at the crossroads, either transition to Socialism or regression into Barbarism." Today, we once more stand at just such a crossroads: ecosocialism or barbarism. Yet this time really is different. Extractive capitalism tears apart the natural systems upon which all life depends and drives the disruption and violence of breakdown hurtling towards us. We are at a terminal juncture.

But we can still rescue our futures. Climate crisis and ecological breakdown are primarily a political crisis. We have the resources, technologies and ideas to decarbonise our economies and bring them within sustainable environmental limits; the challenge is mobilising the power and energy to match the scale of emergency, overcoming entrenched interests and inertia to drive transformation within a narrow time frame.

To do this, we need to replace the economics of extractivism with a twenty-first-century ecosocialism: the collective effort to democratise our economic and political institutions, repurposing them towards social wellbeing and individual flourishing, rooted in an abundant and thriving natural world. It is a goal that demands a different type of economy, one reoriented towards meeting social and environmental needs, overturning the injustices of contemporary societies and an extractive, neo-imperial global political economy; promoting communal luxury in societies of everyday beauty and comfort; expanding social ownership and control; and deepening and extending democracy and freedom. If you do not like the word "ecosocialism," then use something else. But this is the systemic change we need to help us thrive as well as survive.

This is not a project of traditional statism, with success simply measured by the size of the state. It is about reimagining the foundational institutions of production, consumption and exchange, of work and leisure, based on principles of equality, deep freedom and collective empowerment, solidarity, sustainability and democracy. In place of the economics of enclosure and extraction, a twenty-first-century commons founded on collective stewardship; in place of concentrated economic power, a democratised marketplace where capital's monopoly over decision-making is replaced by social control and generative enterprise; against austerity, an ambitious mission-oriented state that lays the foundations for an expanded, decommodified public realm; and a reimagined household economy that dismantles unjust inequalities and increases leisure time.

Extending social control over finance to direct its power to serve real needs, valuing work that nurtures and sustains life, and democratising technological development and use to extend our capacity for creativity and mutual endeavour, ecosocialism builds the conditions for thriving. It works through a new internationalism, recognising that the failed age of the "Washington Consensus" is over, and that, in its place, international cooperation must be built on a full understanding of how we got here and a shared view of where we go next. And it seeks to dismantle the structural racism and class inequalities that blight our societies.

This will require more than marginal adjustments. As signs at Black Lives Matter demonstrations across the world have spelled out, "The system isn't broken, it was built this way." To that end, we need one, two, many Green New Deals—adapted to local needs and cultures—confidently deploying the tools of public investment, democratic ownership, and green industrial strategy to rapidly remake our economies for sustainability and justice. The entwined environmental and inequality emergencies demand unparalleled ambition. Corporate greenwashing, "Green Deals" and limited "green Keynesianism" won't suffice; the scale, complexity and compounding nature of the crisis demand a deeper, planned transition. An ambitious reordering of our economy is needed to secure more sustainable forms of abundance than the partial freedoms, inequalities and environmental crises of extractive capitalism.

If not now, when? The coronavirus pandemic, a profound public health emergency, has triggered the worst economic crisis in recent history. A viral cataclysm emerged from capitalism's entangled and devastating impact on the environment and spread through circuits of global production, falling upon healthcare systems weakened by a decade of austerity. In doing so, it was a warning from the future, a system-wide crisis whose exponential power overwhelmed the linear, outmoded politics of neoliberalism. It is the first crisis of the age of environmental breakdown.

What we propose is a politics for common care, mutual solidarity and joy, one that can renew hope against the deadening grip of the past: against the multiplying financial claims on our economic futures and the accumulated harms of environmental destruction that are now an existential threat to life. The environmental crisis changes everything: we can respond by delivering collective transformation.

This is an edited excerpt from Planet on Fire: A Manifesto for the Age of Environmental Breakdown *by Mathew Lawrence and Laurie Laybourn-Langton (Verso, 2021).*

SUNDAY JULY 24

_____

_____

_____

_____

_____

_____

MONDAY JULY 25

_____

_____

_____

_____

_____

_____

_____

TUESDAY JULY 26

_____

_____

_____

_____

_____

_____

JULY 25, 1846 Henry David Thoreau is jailed for refusing to pay taxes due to his opposition to slavery and the Mexican-American war. "Under a government which imprisons any unjustly, the true place for a just man is also a prison." —CIVIL DISOBEDIENCE

JULY 26, 1953 Fidel Castro leads the Cuban revolution against the US-backed dictator Fulgencio Batista with an attack on the Moncada Barracks. "Condemn me. It does not matter. History will absolve me." —CASTRO, BEFORE BEING SENTENCED FOR THE ATTACK

JULY 26, 1956 Gamal Abdel Nasser, president of Egypt, announces the nationalization of the Suez Canal. "We shall yield neither to force nor the dollar."

JULY 27, 1972 Selma James, cofounder of the International Wages for Housework campaign, and Mariarosa Dalla Costa publish _The Power of Women and the Subversion of the Community_, which identified women's unwaged care work as an essential element of capitalism. "We must refuse housework as women's work, as work imposed upon us, which we never invented, which has never been paid for, in which they have forced us to cope with absurd hours, twelve and thirteen a day, in order to force us to stay at home."

JULY 28, 1794 Maximilien Robespierre, the face of the French Revolution's Reign of Terror, is guillotined without a trial. "The tyrant's trial is insurrection; his judgment is the fall of his power; his penalty, whatever the liberty of the people demands." —"AGAINST GRANTING THE KING A TRIAL"

JULY 29, 1848 The Young Irelander Rebellion of 1848 takes place: a failed Irish nationalist revolt against British rule, sometimes called the Famine Rebellion (since it took place during the Great Irish Famine) or the Battle of Ballingarry.

WEDNESDAY JULY 27

Castro with fellow revolutionary Camilo Cienfuegos entering
Havana, 1959

THURSDAY JULY 28

NOTES:

FRIDAY JULY 29

SATURDAY JULY 30

SUNDAY JULY 31

_____

_____

_____

_____

_____

_____

_____

MONDAY AUGUST 1

_____

_____

_____

_____

_____

_____

TUESDAY AUGUST 2

_____

_____

_____

_____

_____

_____

AUGUST 1, 1933 Anti-Fascist activists Bruno Tesch, Walter Möller, Karl Wolff and August Lütgens executed by the Nazi regime in Altona.

AUGUST 2, 1924 James Baldwin, black American novelist, critic, and essayist, is born in Harlem, New York City. "People can cry much easier than they can change, a rule of psychology people like me picked up as kids on the street." —"JAMES BALDWIN BACK HOME"

AUGUST 3, 1960 Independence Day in the Republic of Niger, marking the nation's independence from France in 1960. Since 1975, it is also Arbor Day, as trees are planted across the nation to aid the fight against desertification.

AUGUST 4, 1983 Revolutionary leader Thomas Sankara assumes power in Burkina Faso, nationalizing mineral wealth and redistributing land. "It took the madmen of yesterday for us to be able to act with extreme clarity today. I want to be one of those madmen. We must dare to invent the future."

AUGUST 5, 1951 Eduardo Chibas, anti-communist Cuban radio personality, shoots himself after his final broadcast. "People of Cuba, keep awake. This is my last knock at your door." —CHIBAS'S LAST WORDS

AUGUST 6, 1969 Theodor Adorno—philosopher, composer and leading member of the Frankfurt School of critical theory—dies. "For the Enlightenment, anything which cannot be resolved into numbers, and ultimately into one, is illusion; modern positivism consigns it to poetry." —DIALECTIC OF ENLIGHTENMENT, CO-AUTHORED WITH MAX HORKHEIMER

AUGUST 6, 2011 Riots break out throughout London after police kill a black man, lasting for several days and leading to more than 3,000 arrests.

WEDNESDAY AUGUST 3

_____

_____

_____

_____

_____

_____

_____

Writer and critic James Baldwin (1924–1987)

THURSDAY AUGUST 4

_____

_____

_____

_____

_____

_____

_____

NOTES:

_____

_____

_____

_____

_____

_____

FRIDAY AUGUST 5

_____

_____

_____

_____

_____

_____

_____

SATURDAY AUGUST 6

_____

_____

_____

_____

_____

_____

_____

SUNDAY AUGUST 7

MONDAY AUGUST 8

TUESDAY AUGUST 9

AUGUST 8, 1961 Wu Han, a member of a dissident group of Chinese intellectuals, writes a play indirectly critical of Mao and the Great Leap Forward, for which he is imprisoned.

> "You pay lip service to the principle
> that the people are the roots of the state.
> But officials still oppress the masses
> while pretending to be virtuous men."
> —"HAI JUI'S DISMISSAL"

AUGUST 8, 1988 Rangoon students call openly for democracy, sparking the 8888 Uprising that toppled Burma's Ne Win government before being violently crushed by government troops.

AUGUST 9, 1650 The English Parliament passes an act outlawing "blasphemous" sects like the Ranters, one of the most radical to emerge during the English Revolution, which denied the authority of churches, priests, and writ.

AUGUST 11, 1828 The first Working Men's Party of the United States is founded in Philadelphia. "And for the support of this declaration, we mutually pledge to each other our faithful aid to the end of our lives." —GEORGE HENRY EVANS, "PARTY DECLARATION OF INDEPENDENCE"

WEDNESDAY AUGUST 10

_____
_____
_____
_____
_____
_____
_____

THURSDAY AUGUST 11

_____
_____
_____
_____
_____
_____

FRIDAY AUGUST 12

_____
_____
_____
_____
_____
_____

SATURDAY AUGUST 13

_____
_____
_____
_____
_____
_____

NOTES:

_____
_____
_____
_____
_____
_____
_____
_____
_____
_____
_____
_____
_____
_____

SUNDAY AUGUST 14

MONDAY AUGUST 15

TUESDAY AUGUST 16

AUGUST 14, 1980 Polish shipyard workers strike to protest the firing of worker Anna Walentynowicz and for the right to form unions. Walentynowicz is reinstated, and several weeks later, the first independent labor union in a Soviet bloc country, Solidarność, is formed, precipitating the fall of the Polish communist regime. "It was the end of the utopian dream, and it enabled us to dismantle the dictatorship by negotiation." —ACTIVIST ADAM MICHNIK

AUGUST 15, 1947 India becomes independent after 200 years of British colonial rule. "A moment comes, which comes but rarely in history, when we step out from the old to the new, when an age ends, and when the soul of a nation, long suppressed, finds utterance." —MOVEMENT LEADER AND INDIA'S FIRST PRIME MINISTER JAWAHARLAL NEHRU, "TRYST WITH DESTINY"

AUGUST 16, 1819 The English cavalry charges into a crowd of over 60,000 rallying in Manchester for parliamentary reform in what becomes known as the Peterloo Massacre.

"Rise like lions after slumber
In unvanquishable number!
Shake your chains to earth like dew
Which in sleep had fallen on you:
Ye are many—they are few!"

—PERCY BYSSHE SHELLEY'S "THE MASQUE OF ANARCHY,"
AN EARLY STATEMENT OF NONVIOLENT RESISTANCE

AUGUST 19, 1953 Mohammad Mosaddegh, the popular, democratically elected prime minister of Iran, is overthrown by a CIA-backed coup. "My greatest sin is that I nationalized Iran's oil industry and discarded the system of political and economic exploitation by the world's greatest empire." —SPEECH AT HIS TRIAL

WEDNESDAY AUGUST 17

_____

_____

_____

_____

_____

_____

_____

A painting of the Peterloo Massacre circulated in pro-suffrage papers, 1819

THURSDAY AUGUST 18

_____

_____

_____

_____

_____

_____

_____

NOTES:

_____

_____

_____

_____

_____

_____

FRIDAY AUGUST 19

_____

_____

_____

_____

_____

_____

_____

SATURDAY AUGUST 20

_____

_____

_____

_____

_____

_____

SUNDAY AUGUST 21

_____

_____

_____

_____

_____

_____

_____

MONDAY AUGUST 22

_____

_____

_____

_____

_____

_____

_____

TUESDAY AUGUST 23

_____

_____

_____

_____

_____

_____

_____

AUGUST 21, 1791 A rebellion against slavery breaks out in Saint Domingue, leading to the Haitian Revolution, the only slave revolt against European colonialists that successfully achieved an independent state. "We seek only to bring men to the liberty that God has given them, and that other men have taken from them only by transgressing His immutable will." —REVOLUTIONARY LEADER TOUSSAINT L'OUVERTURE

AUGUST 21, 1940 Leon Trotsky, Marxist revolutionary and theorist, is assassinated by Soviet agents. "Life is beautiful. Let the future generations cleanse it of all evil, oppression and violence, and enjoy it to the full." —"TROTSKY'S TESTAMENT," WRITTEN MONTHS EARLIER

AUGUST 23, 1572 French Catholics, incited by the monarchy, kill thousands of Protestants (known as Huguenots) in the St. Bartholomew's Day Massacre, giving rise to the Monarchomachs, a movement supporting tyrannicide.

AUGUST 23, 1927 During the Red Scare—a period of intense political repression in the US—the Italian-born anarchists Nicola Sacco and Bartolomeo Vanzetti are wrongfully convicted and executed for robbery and murder.

AUGUST 25, 1968 Yippies—the Youth International Party, which brought counterculture theatricality to the US antiwar and New Left movements—host their Festival of Life at the Democratic National Convention in Chicago, leading to police actions and a trial for conspiracy to riot for the organizers. "There will be public fornication whenever and wherever there is an aroused appendage and willing apertures." —ACTIVIST ED SANDERS, "PREDICTIONS FOR YIPPIE ACTIVITIES"

WEDNESDAY AUGUST 24

_____

_____

_____

_____

_____

_____

_____

Declaration of the Rights of Man and of the Citizen, painted by Jean-Jacques-François Le Barbier

THURSDAY AUGUST 25

_____

_____

_____

_____

_____

_____

_____

NOTES:

_____

_____

_____

_____

_____

_____

FRIDAY AUGUST 26

_____

_____

_____

_____

_____

_____

_____

SATURDAY AUGUST 27

_____

_____

_____

_____

_____

_____

NO DEATHS, THAT WAS THE MAIN THING:
NO DEATHS
JOSEPH ANDRAS

She pulls up. Get out here, this car shouldn't be seen near the factory. Good luck. He gets out of the car and waves. Jacqueline waves back and steps on the gas. Fernand adjusts his sports bag on his shoulder. Pale green, the strap lighter in color next to the drawstring opening, borrowed from a friend who uses it when he plays basketball on Sundays. Look as natural as possible. Like nothing's going on, nothing at all. For the past few days he's been taking it to work, to get the security guards used to it. Fernand is thinking about the bomb at the bottom of the bag, the bomb and its tick-tock tick-tock. It's two o'clock, the time has come to return to the machines. I'm coming, just putting my bag down, be right there, Mo, yes, see you in a sec.

Fernand glances around the yard, keeping his head still as he does so. As natural as possible. No sudden movements. He walks slowly toward the abandoned shed he scoped out three weeks ago. The factory's gas holder was inaccessible: you'd need to get past barbed wire and security guards, posted at three different points along the way.

Worse than a city-center bank or a presidential palace (not to mention that you have to strip off all, or almost all, your clothes before they let you through). Impossible, in short. And dangerous, much too dangerous, he had said to comrade Hachelaf. No deaths, that was the main thing: no deaths. Better that little storeroom where nobody ever goes. The old worker, Matahar, his mustard-colored head the texture of crumpled paper, gave him the key without the slightest suspicion—just need to take a nap, Matahar, I'll give it back to you tomorrow, don't tell the others, promise? The old man was as good as his word, العظيـــم والله, I'll never say anything to anyone, Fernand, you can sleep tight. He takes the key out of his pocket, turns it in the lock, glances behind him, no one, he enters, opens the cupboard, puts the sports bag on the middle shelf, closes the door and turns the key again. Then goes around to the factory's main entrance, greets the security guard as usual, and approaches his machine tool. It's stopped raining, did you see, Mo? He did indeed, awful weather, this, been gray and doing whatever all November.

Fernand sits at his station and puts on his gloves, worn out at the seams. A contact, whose first and last names he does not know, will be waiting for him when the factory closes at seven, that is, just before the bomb goes off. That person will take him to a hideout in the Casbah somewhere, he doesn't know where exactly, and from there he will hook up with the guerrillas ... The next day, maybe, or in a few days—not his decision. He has to wait patiently for his turn to leave, every day, at the same time as everyone else, put down his worn-out green gloves, every day, joke a little with his friends and see you tomorrow, that's right, g'night guys, say hello to the family for me. Don't raise any suspicions: that's what Hachelaf kept telling him. Much as he tries not to, he keeps thinking about Hélène. He's not doing anything else, in fact—his brain, that three-pound brat, has a taste for melodrama. How will she react when she finds out that her husband has left Algiers and gone underground? Does she suspect? Was it such a good idea to keep this a secret? His comrades certainly thought so. The struggle forces love to keep a low profile, ideals require sacrifices, no room for soft hearts in this fight ... Yes, it was for the best, for the smooth running of the operation.

It is almost four o'clock when someone calls him from behind. Fernand turns around in response to the question mark punctuating his name. Cops. Damn.

This is a revised extract from Tomorrow They Won't Dare to Murder Us: A Novel *by Joseph Andras and translated from the French by Simon Leser (Verso, 2021).*

SUNDAY AUGUST 28

_____

_____

_____

_____

_____

_____

_____

MONDAY AUGUST 29

_____

_____

_____

_____

_____

_____

_____

TUESDAY AUGUST 30

_____

_____

_____

_____

_____

_____

_____

AUGUST 29, 1786 Poor farmers crushed by debt and taxes rise up in armed rebellion in Massachusetts, US, in what came to be known as Shay's Rebellion. "The great men are going to get all we have and I think it is time for us to rise and put a stop to it, and have no more courts, nor sheriffs, nor collectors, nor lawyers." —PLOUGH JOGGER, FARMER, SPEAKING AT THE ILLEGAL CONVENTION OPPOSING THE MASSACHUSETTS LEGISLATURE

AUGUST 29, 1844 Edward Carpenter, pioneering socialist poet, philosopher, and early homosexual thinker, is born in England. "It has become clear that the number of individuals affected with 'sexual inversion' in some degree or other is very great—much greater than is generally supposed to be the case." —HOMOGENIC LOVE

SEPTEMBER 1, 1961 The Eritrean struggle for independence begins when members of the Eritrean Liberation Front fire first shots on the occupying Ethiopian army.

"What have I done
That you deny me my torch?"
—"SHIGEY HABUNI," POPULAR SONG WITH TIES TO THE NATIONALIST MOVEMENT

SEPTEMBER 3, 2017 Private security guards for the Dakota Access Pipeline unleash dogs on indigenous water protectors near the Standing Rock Sioux Tribe reservation in North Dakota. A protest encampment, established months earlier, quickly swelled to become the largest gathering of Native Americans in recent history. "Mní Wičoni— Water is Life." —SLOGAN

WEDNESDAY AUGUST 31

_____

_____

_____

_____

_____

_____

_____

Standing Rock Sioux Tribe reservation logo, 1873

THURSDAY SEPTEMBER 1

_____

_____

_____

_____

_____

_____

_____

NOTES:

_____

_____

_____

_____

_____

_____

FRIDAY SEPTEMBER 2

_____

_____

_____

_____

_____

_____

SATURDAY SEPTEMBER 3

_____

_____

_____

_____

_____

_____

SUNDAY SEPTEMBER 4

MONDAY SEPTEMBER 5

TUESDAY SEPTEMBER 6

SEPTEMBER 6, 1960 "Manifesto of the 121" is signed by French intellectuals (including Jean-Paul Sartre, Maurice Blanchot, and others), supporting the right of Algerians to fight for independence from the French. "Must we be reminded that fifteen years after the destruction of the Hitlerite order, French militarism has managed to bring back torture and restore it as an institution in Europe?"

SEPTEMBER 7, 1872 Russian revolutionary and anarchist theorist Mikhail Bakunin is expelled from the First International, presaging a split between the anarchist and Marxist factions of the workers' movement. "If you took the most ardent revolutionary, vested him in absolute power, within a year he would be worse than the Tsar himself." —BAKUNIN ON AUTHORITARIAN SOCIALISM

SEPTEMBER 8, 1965 Delano Grape Strike begins in California when Filipino grape pickers walk out and ask Cesar Chavez, leader of the mostly Latino National Farm Workers Association, to join them. The campaign ended five years later in success, largely due to a consumer boycott. "Time accomplishes for the poor what money does for the rich." —CHAVEZ, "LETTER FROM DELANO"

SEPTEMBER 9, 869 Ali ibn Muhammad, a leader of the Zanj uprising of African slaves against the Abbasid Caliphate in Iraq, begins freeing slaves and gaining adherents. "Ali ordered their slaves to bring whips of palm branches and, while their masters and agents were prostrated on the ground, each one was given five hundred lashes." —PERSIAN HISTORIAN IBN JARIR AL-TABARI

SEPTEMBER 9, 1739 Stono Rebellion, the largest slave uprising in Britain's mainland North American colonies, led by a slave called Jemmy, erupts near Charleston, South Carolina. Over the next two years, slave uprisings occurred independently in Georgia and South Carolina.

WEDNESDAY SEPTEMBER 7

_____

_____

_____

_____

_____

_____

_____

Cesar Chavez (1927–1993) following the successful farmworker strike and consumer grape boycott, 1970

THURSDAY SEPTEMBER 8

_____

_____

_____

_____

_____

_____

_____

NOTES:

_____

_____

_____

_____

_____

_____

FRIDAY SEPTEMBER 9

_____

_____

_____

_____

_____

_____

_____

SATURDAY SEPTEMBER 10

_____

_____

_____

_____

_____

_____

SUNDAY SEPTEMBER 11

_____

_____

_____

_____

_____

_____

MONDAY SEPTEMBER 12

_____

_____

_____

_____

_____

_____

_____

TUESDAY SEPTEMBER 13

_____

_____

_____

_____

_____

_____

_____

SEPTEMBER 14, 1791 Olympe de Gouges publishes the _Declaration of the Rights of Women and the Female Citizen_, one of the first tracts to champion women's rights. "Woman is born free and remains the equal of man in rights."

SEPTEMBER 15, 1889 Claude McKay, Harlem Renaissance poet and delegate to the Third International, is born in Jamaica.

"If we must die—O let us nobly die!
So that our precious blood may not be shed
In vain; then even the monsters we defy
Shall be constrained to honor us though dead!"

—"IF WE MUST DIE"

SEPTEMBER 16, 1810 Miguel Hidalgo, a priest in Dolores, Mexico, issues a call to revolt against Spanish rule, setting in motion the Mexican War of Independence. "My children: a new dispensation come to us today. Will you receive it? Will you free yourselves?"

SEPTEMBER 16, 1923 Alongside her lover and his six-year-old nephew, Ito Noe, anarchist and feminist writer and activist, is brutally murdered by Japanese police. The event, known as the Amakasu Incident, sparked outrage throughout Japan and led to a ten-year sentence for the officer.

SEPTEMBER 16, 1973 Victor Jara, Chilean poet and songwriter, is tortured and killed in Chile Stadium following Pinochet's coup against Allende.

"How hard is it to sing
when I must sing of horror"

—"ESTADIO CHILE," WRITTEN BY JARA IN THE STADIUM AND SMUGGLED OUT INSIDE A SHOE

WEDNESDAY SEPTEMBER 14

Ito Noe, Japanese anarchist and feminist

THURSDAY SEPTEMBER 15

NOTES:

FRIDAY SEPTEMBER 16

SATURDAY SEPTEMBER 17

SUNDAY SEPTEMBER 18

MONDAY SEPTEMBER 19

TUESDAY SEPTEMBER 20

SEPTEMBER 19, 1921 The Brazilian educator and philosopher Paulo Freire is born. His *Pedagogy of the Oppressed* infuses a classical theory of education with Marxist and anticolonialist approaches. "This, then, is the great humanistic and historical task of the oppressed: to liberate themselves and their oppressors as well."

SEPTEMBER 21, 1956 Nicaraguan poet Rigoberto López Pérez assassinates Anastasio Somoza García, the longtime dictator of Nicaragua, before being killed himself. "Seeing that all efforts to return Nicaragua to being (or to becoming for the first time) a free country without shame or stain have been futile, I have decided that I should be the one to try to initiate the beginning of the end of this tyranny." —LETTER TO HIS MOTHER

SEPTEMBER 23, 1884 Liberal party partisans occupy a mountaintop in Kabasan, Japan, in a rebellion against the Meiji government.

"Yet while we lament, asking
why our insignificant selves
were oppressed,
the rain still falls
heavily on the people."
—PARTICIPANT OHASHI GENZABURO

SEPTEMBER 24, 1838 A meeting held on Kersal Moor in England launches the Chartist movement, the first mass working-class movement in Europe.
—THE PEOPLE'S CHARTER AND PETITION

WEDNESDAY SEPTEMBER 21

_____

_____

_____

_____

_____

_____

_____

Great Chartist Meeting on Kennington Common, London in 1848

THURSDAY SEPTEMBER 22

_____

_____

_____

_____

_____

_____

_____

NOTES:

_____

_____

_____

_____

_____

_____

FRIDAY SEPTEMBER 23

_____

_____

_____

_____

_____

_____

_____

SATURDAY SEPTEMBER 24

_____

_____

_____

_____

_____

_____

_____

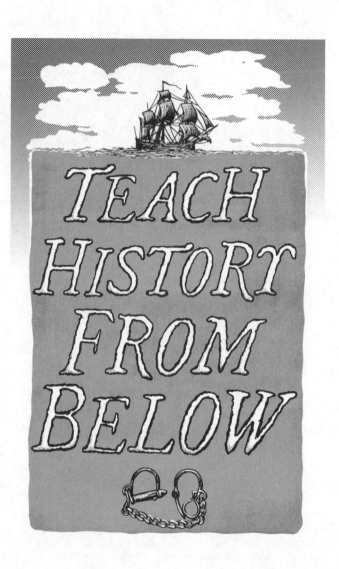

Teach History From Below by Shaun Slifer
(Justseeds Artists' Cooperative/justseeds.org)

UNDER THE BURNING COP CARS, (A WORLD WHERE THE SAFETY OF THE FEW IS NOT AT THE EXPENSE OF THE MANY) THE BEACH.

Under the Burning Cop Cars by Josh MacPhee
(Justseeds Artists' Cooperative/justseeds.org)

SUNDAY SEPTEMBER 25

SEPTEMBER 26, 1940 Fleeing Vichy France, Marxist theorist Walter Benjamin is threatened with deportation from Spain and kills himself with morphine tablets.

SEPTEMBER 28, 1829 David Walker, a contributor to the first African-American newspaper *Freedom Journal*, publishes his "Appeal to the Colored Citizens of the World," calling for slaves to revolt against their masters. Southern plantation owners respond by putting a $3,000 bounty on his head. "The whites want slaves, and want us for their slaves, but some of them will curse the day they ever saw us."

MONDAY SEPTEMBER 26

SEPTEMBER 1875 Senator William Allison arrives in Sioux country to negotiate a land lease agreement with the Native Americans that would have allowed the United States government to mine the area for gold. His proposal is met with 300 mounted warriors, led by Little Big Man, who chant the song below in response.

"The Black Hills is my land and I love it
And whoever interferes
Will hear this gun."
—SIOUX WARRIORS' SONG

TUESDAY SEPTEMBER 27

SEPTEMBER 30, 1935 The anti-Stalinist Workers' Party of Marxist Unification (POUM) is founded in Spain, where it is especially active during the Civil War. "The totalitarian states can do great things, but there is one thing they cannot do: they cannot give the factory-worker a rifle and tell him to take it home and keep it in his bedroom. That rifle hanging on the wall of the working-class flat or laborer's cottage is the symbol of democracy."
—POUM MEMBER GEORGE ORWELL, ARTICLE IN THE *EVENING STANDARD*

WEDNESDAY SEPTEMBER 28

Little Big Man—an Oglala Lakota, or Oglala Sioux, leader

THURSDAY SEPTEMBER 29

NOTES:

FRIDAY SEPTEMBER 30

SATURDAY OCTOBER 1

SUNDAY OCTOBER 2

MONDAY OCTOBER 3

TUESDAY OCTOBER 4

OCTOBER 5, 1877 Nez Perce leader Hinmatóowy-alahtq'it, also known as Chief Joseph, ends a legendary three-month flight to Canada by surrendering to US forces. "Do not misunderstand me, but understand fully with reference to my affection for the land. I never said the land was mine to do with as I choose. The one who has a right to dispose of it is the one who created it." —"AN INDIAN'S VIEW OF INDIAN AFFAIRS"

OCTOBER 5, 1959 Robert F. Williams's Black Armed Guard fires on Ku Klux Klan members riding past a member's house in North Carolina. "Nowhere in the annals of history does the record show a people delivered from bondage by patience alone." —"WE MUST FIGHT BACK"

OCTOBER 6, 1985 Riots break out on the Broadwater Farm estate in one of London's poorest neighborhoods, a day after an Afro-Caribbean woman died of heart failure during a police search. One police officer was killed.

OCTOBER 7, 1979 Landless farmers occupy the Macali land in Ronda Alta, Brazil, leading to the founding of the Landless Workers Movement (MST). "This is what I've always wanted: 'to overcome, to overcome.'" —MST LEADER MIGUEL ALVES DOS SANTOS

OCTOBER 8, 1969 The Weather Underground, a faction of the Students for a Democratic Society, stages the first of its "Days of Rage," a series of confrontations with the Chicago police in 1969. "Freaks are revolutionaries and revolutionaries are freaks. If you want to find us, this is where we are." —"COMMUNIQUÉ #1"

WEDNESDAY OCTOBER 5

FBI "Wanted" poster for civil rights activist Robert F. Williams (1925–1996)

THURSDAY OCTOBER 6

NOTES:

FRIDAY OCTOBER 7

SATURDAY OCTOBER 8

SUNDAY OCTOBER 9

_____

_____

_____

_____

_____

_____

_____

_____

_____

MONDAY OCTOBER 10

_____

_____

_____

_____

_____

_____

_____

_____

TUESDAY OCTOBER 11

_____

_____

_____

_____

_____

_____

_____

_____

OCTOBER 10, 1903 British activist Emmeline Pankhurst cofounds the Women's Social and Political Union, a militant all-women suffragist organization dedicated to "deeds, not words." "The moving spirit of militancy is deep and abiding reverence for human life." —*MY OWN STORY*

OCTOBER 10, 1911 The Wuchang Uprising begins after the Qing government suppresses political protest against the handover of local railways to foreign ventures. Quickly spreading through China, the Xinhai Revolution took down the 2,100-year-old dynastic empire within months.

OCTOBER 10, 1947 Senegalese railway workers begin a strike that lasted months, in what would become a watershed moment in Senegal's anticolonial struggle. "It rolled out over its own length, like the movement of a serpent. It was as long as a life." —*GOD'S BITS OF WOOD*, A NOVEL BY FILMMAKER, WRITER, AND ACTIVIST OUSMANE SEMBÈNE BASED ON THE STRIKE

OCTOBER 15, 1966 The Black Panther Party is founded in Oakland, California. "The people make revolution; the oppressors, by their brutal actions, cause resistance by the people. The vanguard party only teaches the correct methods of resistance." —COFOUNDER HUEY P. NEWTON, "THE CORRECT HANDLING OF A REVOLUTION"

OCTOBER 15, 1968 The Jamaican government bans the Guyanese scholar and Black Power activist Walter Rodney from the country, sparking what became known as the Rodney Riots. "The only great men among the unfree and the oppressed are those who struggle to destroy the oppressor." —*HOW EUROPE UNDERDEVELOPED AFRICA*

WEDNESDAY OCTOBER 12

Black Panthers demonstrating outside of the Washington State
Capitol Building, 1969

THURSDAY OCTOBER 13

NOTES:

FRIDAY OCTOBER 14

SATURDAY OCTOBER 15

SUNDAY OCTOBER 16

_____
_____
_____
_____
_____
_____
_____
_____

MONDAY OCTOBER 17

_____
_____
_____
_____
_____
_____

TUESDAY OCTOBER 18

_____
_____
_____
_____
_____
_____
_____

OCTOBER 17, 1961 Algerian demonstrators in Paris, denouncing France's colonial war in their home country, are met with force. An estimated 300 were massacred; the French government acknowledges forty victims.

OCTOBER 18, 1899 The Battle of Senluo Temple breaks out in northern China between government forces and the Militia United in Righteousness—known in English as the "Boxers" for their strict martial arts regimen—in what would eventually become the Boxer Rebellion, an anti-foreign and anti-Christian uprising.

"When at last all the Foreign Devils
are expelled to the very last man,
The Great Qing, united, together,
will bring peace to this our land"
—BOXERS WALL POSTER

OCTOBER 19, 1986 Samora Machel, Mozambican revolutionary leader and post-independence president, dies in a plane crash in South Africa.

OCTOBER 21, 1956 Dedan Kimathi, leader of Kenya's Mau Mau Uprising, is captured by a British colonial officer later nicknamed the "Butcher of Bahrain." "I lead them because God never created any nation to be ruled by another nation forever."

OCTOBER 22, 1964 Jean-Paul Sartre refuses to accept the Nobel Prize for Literature. "The writer must therefore refuse to let himself be transformed into an institution." —LETTER TO THE NOBEL COMMITTEE

WEDNESDAY OCTOBER 19

A Chinese "Boxer," 1900

THURSDAY OCTOBER 20

NOTES:

FRIDAY OCTOBER 21

SATURDAY OCTOBER 22

V

SILICON VALLEY AND THE WAR ON SEX

JILLIAN C. YORK

At a time when attitudes toward sex work, transgender individuals, and other sexual minorities are by and large changing for the better, it is perhaps ironic that Silicon Valley's CEOs are so rapidly closing off the spaces where such communities have long gathered. Or maybe it's not right to describe it in ironic terms—after all, the disregard for these spaces has been accompanied by an agenda of rapid growth in San Francisco that has all but closed down the city's legendary queer spaces so that Silicon Valley's highly paid workers can drink $7 cups of coffee and dine at the latest hip restaurants.

Millennials and their younger counterparts are redefining sex, sexuality, and gender norms and claiming public space for marginalized identities, whilst Silicon Valley's values seem remarkably regressive. If these platforms are the new terrain for long-standing debates about the content and character of public discourse, what does it say about our society that they have the tolerance of a nineteenth-century priest? Moreover, what effect will it have on future generations? What does it mean that

we're encouraged to spend every waking hour on these platforms but can't be ourselves on them? Furthermore, in requiring creators to stay within the lines or risk self-censorship, are we creating an archive of sexuality for the future that hardly resembles our current—and far more permissive—reality?

I cannot help but think about what was lost when the Nazis seized power, decimating the freedoms that had flourished in the Weimar Republic. In that unique and brief period of history, Berlin was a hotspot of queer activity, from nightclubs to political organizing. There were numerous queer publications, including *The Third Sex*, most likely the world's first transgender magazine. Sex work was mostly legal. And, of course, there was the Institut für Sexualwissenschaft, a sexology institute that advocated for LGBT rights, among other things.

Perhaps the Weimar Republic comes to mind because, one hundred years later, my home city of Berlin is once again flourishing in its sexual freedoms while also facing the threat of right-wing populism. Or perhaps it's

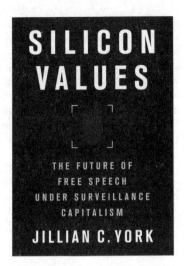

because, while these companies cannot and should not be directly compared to the Nazis, they wield the same prudish and authoritarian tendencies when it comes to sexual freedom. And I fear that, without intervention, we will see the erasure of our living history in quite the same way our ancestors did a century ago.

These are important concerns that affect society as a whole, and they deserve a more prominent place in the public discourse. But, as I seek to illustrate, it is the most vulnerable members of society who suffer the most from bad policy. Unsurprisingly, the most marginalized members of society are rarely invited to the table to lend their views as policy is being created—and when they do speak out after the fact, they're often ignored. "Think about social media as the real world," says Kali Sudhra (an activist, sex worker, and educator who works to give voice to sex and porn workers of color), who says that the people that face

the most discrimination are "trans folk, Black and Indigenous people of color, sex workers and people living with disabilities." Those who make the rules—whether lawmakers or corporate executives—rarely engage in social media use to the same degree as the communities Sudhra mentions, because they don't have to. The ruling class has money, and access to the *New York Times* opinion page—they do not need to rely on Twitter to get their voices heard. To them, social media is not real life, and their online acquaintances aren't members of their communities.

But for some, access to online platforms can mean everything. "I can pretty confidently say that I do not think I would've transitioned if it weren't for Tumblr," Courtney Demone told me, and she is not the only one. Countless queer friends have, over the years, told me that online platforms, and the connections made through them, are what helped them understand their identities. It is true for me, too. If I had not had access to online bulletin boards from a young age, I too might not have learned the terms that helped me find my own sexual identity until I was in college. I believe that those at the top know how much online platforms can mean to people like Demone and me. I believe that they have spent at least some time thinking about the consequences of restricting certain types of vital speech. So what conclusion can I possibly arrive at other than that they have simply put profit before people?

This is an edited excerpt from Silicon Values: The Future of Free Speech under Surveillance Capitalism *by Jillian C. York (Verso, 2021).*

SUNDAY OCTOBER 23

_____

_____

_____

_____

_____

_____

_____

MONDAY OCTOBER 24

_____

_____

_____

_____

_____

_____

_____

TUESDAY OCTOBER 25

_____

_____

_____

_____

_____

_____

OCTOBER 23, 1850 First National Women's Rights Convention meets in Worcester, Massachusetts. The following year, poet and journalist Elizabeth Oakes Smith is nominated as its president, only to be rejected after showing up in a dress baring her neck and arms. "Do we fully understand that we aim at nothing less than an entire subversion of the existing order of society, a dissolution of the whole existing social compact?"

OCTOBER 27, 1967 The 1967 Abortion Act was passed in the United Kingdom, legalizing abortions for up to 28 weeks. Women in Northern Ireland continue to be excluded from access to this healthcare in their own country.

OCTOBER 28, 1647 The Putney Debates begin, in which members of the New Model Army, who had recently seized London, debate Britain's new constitution. "The poorest man in England is not bound in a strict sense to that government that he hath not had a voice to put himself under." —LEVELLERS SUPPORTER COLONEL RAINSBOROUGH ARGUING FOR UNIVERSAL MALE SUFFRAGE

OCTOBER 29, 1888 Li Dazhao, librarian, intellectual, and cofounder of the Chinese Communist Party, is born. "China is a rural nation and most of the laboring class consists of peasants. Unless they are liberated, our whole nation will not be liberated." —"DEVELOP THE PEASANTRY"

OCTOBER 29, 1956 Israel invades Egypt after its nationalization of the Suez Canal, followed a few days later by UK and French troops; they are met with local resistance.

"Not through hope will the prize be taken,
The world is taken by struggle."
   —THE "DIVA OF THE EAST" UMM KULTHUM'S POPULAR
   SONG "EGYPT SPEAKS OF HERSELF," WHICH COULD BE
   HEARD RINGING THROUGH THE STREETS

WEDNESDAY OCTOBER 26

Chinese comintern Li Dazhao (1888–1927)

THURSDAY OCTOBER 27

NOTES:

FRIDAY OCTOBER 28

SATURDAY OCTOBER 29

SUNDAY OCTOBER 30

MONDAY OCTOBER 31

TUESDAY NOVEMBER 1

OCTOBER 30, 1969 The Kenya People's Union is banned, transforming the country into a one-party state; its leader, the Luo chief and first vice president of independent Kenya Oginga Odinga, is detained. "We fought for *uhuru* so that people may rule themselves. Direct action, not underhand diplomacy and silent intrigue by professional politicians, won *uhuru*, and only popular mobilization can make it meaningful."
—*NOT YET UHURU*

OCTOBER 31, 1517 Martin Luther composes his letter to the Catholic Church, the *95 Theses*, which quickly spread across Europe and spark the Protestant Reformation. "He who sees a man in need, and passes him by, and gives [his money] for pardons, purchases not the indulgences of the pope, but the indignation of God."

NOVEMBER 1811 A letter sent from "Ned Ludd" in Nottingham, England, threatens to break the looms of a property owner, in an early document from the Luddite Uprising.

> "The guilty may fear but no vengeance he aims
> At the honest man's life or Estate"
>
> —LUDDITES, "GENERAL LUDDS TRIUMPH"

NOVEMBER 4, 1780 Quechua leader Túpac Amaru II leads an indigenous rebellion against Spanish control of Peru, beginning with the capture and killing of the Spanish governor by his slave. "There are no accomplices here but you and I. You the oppressor and I the liberator. Both of us deserve to die." —TÚPAC AMARU II, LAST WORDS TO GENERAL JOSÉ ANTONIO DE ARECHE

WEDNESDAY NOVEMBER 2

Martin Luther (1529) by Lucas Cranach the Elder

THURSDAY NOVEMBER 3

FRIDAY NOVEMBER 4

SATURDAY NOVEMBER 5

SUNDAY NOVEMBER 6

_____

_____

_____

_____

_____

_____

_____

MONDAY NOVEMBER 7

_____

_____

_____

_____

_____

_____

TUESDAY NOVEMBER 8

_____

_____

_____

_____

_____

_____

_____

NOVEMBER 7, 1917 Lenin leads the Bolsheviks in revolution against the provisional Russian government, establishing what will become the Soviet Union. "Freedom in capitalist society always remains about the same as it was in the ancient Greek republics: freedom for the slave-owners."
—THE STATE AND REVOLUTION

NOVEMBER 8, 1775 Thomas Spence, English radical and advocate for common ownership of land, delivers a speech with one of the earliest uses of the term "Rights of Man."

"Ye landlords vile, whose man's place mar,
  Come levy rents here if you can;
  Your stewards and lawyers I defy,
  And live with all the RIGHTS OF MAN"
    —"THE REAL RIGHTS OF MAN"

NOVEMBER 8, 1926 Antonio Gramsci, leader of the Italian Communist Party, is arrested by Mussolini and sentenced to twenty years in prison, during which time he would write his famous _Prison Notebooks_. "'Vanguards' without armies to back them up, 'commandos' without infantry or artillery, these too are transpositions from the language of rhetorical heroism." —"VOLUNTARISM AND SOCIAL MASSES"

NOVEMBER 10, 1995 Nigerian government hangs Ken Saro-Wiwa and the rest of the Ogoni Nine for their campaigning against the oil industry, and especially Royal Dutch Shell. "Dance your anger and your joys; dance the military guns to silence; dance their dumb laws to the dump; dance oppression and injustice to death; dance the end of Shell's ecological war of thirty years."
—STATEMENT OF THE OGONI PEOPLE TO THE TENTH SESSION OF THE WORKING GROUP IN INDIGENOUS POPULATIONS

WEDNESDAY NOVEMBER 9

Lenin speaking at an assembly of Red Army troops bound for the
Polish front, with Trotsky at the base, Moscow, 1920

THURSDAY NOVEMBER 10

NOTES:

FRIDAY NOVEMBER 11

SATURDAY NOVEMBER 12

SUNDAY NOVEMBER 13

_____

_____

_____

_____

_____

_____

_____

MONDAY NOVEMBER 14

_____

_____

_____

_____

_____

_____

_____

TUESDAY NOVEMBER 15

_____

_____

_____

_____

_____

_____

NOVEMBER 15, 1781 Túpac Katari, Aymara leader of an army that laid siege to the Spanish colonial city of La Paz, Bolivia, is betrayed and killed. "I die but will return tomorrow as thousand thousands." —KATARI'S LAST WORDS

NOVEMBER 15, 1988 Palestinian Declaration of Independence, written by poet Mahmoud Darwish, is proclaimed.

NOVEMBER 16, 1885 Louis Riel, Métis leader who headed two rebellions against a Canadian incursion into their territory, is hanged for treason. "I will perhaps be one day acknowledged as more than a leader of the half-breeds, and if I am I will have an opportunity of being acknowledged as a leader of good in this great country." —RIEL'S FINAL STATEMENT TO THE JURY

NOVEMBER 19, 1915 Joe Hill, militant songwriter and organizer with the International Workers of the World, is executed by firing squad. "Don't waste any time in mourning—organize." —HILL'S FAREWELL LETTER TO BILL HAYWOOD

NOVEMBER 19, 1979 Angela Davis—black feminist, philosopher, and prison abolitionist—wins the vice presidential nomination for the US Communist Party. "Prisons do not disappear problems, they disappear human beings. And the practice of disappearing vast numbers of people from poor, immigrant, and racially marginalized communities has literally become big business." —"MASKED RACISM"

WEDNESDAY NOVEMBER 16

Angela Davis on her first visit to the Soviet Union, 1972

THURSDAY NOVEMBER 17

NOTES:

FRIDAY NOVEMBER 18

SATURDAY NOVEMBER 19

SUNDAY NOVEMBER 20

_____

_____

_____

_____

_____

_____

_____

_____

MONDAY NOVEMBER 21

_____

_____

_____

_____

_____

_____

_____

TUESDAY NOVEMBER 22

_____

_____

_____

_____

_____

_____

_____

_____

NOVEMBER 20, 1969 The Native American group Indians of All Tribes occupies Alcatraz island in the San Francisco Bay and holds it for fourteen months. "Alcatraz Island is more than suitable as an Indian Reservation, as determined by the white man's own standards." —ALCATRAZ PROCLAMATION

NOVEMBER 24, 1947 House Un-American Activities Committee votes to hold the "Hollywood Ten," a group of writers and directors blacklisted for their communist affiliations, in contempt of Congress. "We are men of peace, we are men who work and we want no quarrel. But if you destroy our peace, if you take away our work, if you try to range us one against the other, we will know what to do." —SPARTACUS SCREENWRITER DALTON TRUMBO'S ANTIWAR NOVEL, _JOHNNY GOT HIS GUN_

NOVEMBER 24, 2014 A white police officer is acquitted in the shooting death of an unarmed black teenager, Michael Brown, in Ferguson, Missouri, setting off protests nationwide under the moniker Black Lives Matter.

NOVEMBER 25, 1832 Abd al-Qader al-Jaza'iri, Sufi and Muslim scholar and Algerian resistance leader, is elected emir of a confederation of tribes that banded together and fought the French invaders for over a decade. "If we leave them alone, they will assault us."

NOVEMBER 25, 1911 Mexican revolutionary Emiliano Zapata proclaims his Plan de Ayala, laying out his ideology and program of land reform, whose slogan "Land and Freedom!" was a watchword of the Mexican Revolution. "The nation is tired of false men and traitors who make promises like liberators and who on arriving in power forget them and constitute themselves as tyrants."

WEDNESDAY NOVEMBER 23

Black Lives Matter protest against police brutality, 2015

THURSDAY NOVEMBER 24

NOTES:

FRIDAY NOVEMBER 25

SATURDAY NOVEMBER 26

THE LIMITS OF POLICE REFORM
ALEX S. VITALE

What we really need is to rethink the role of police in society. The origins and function of the police are intimately tied to the management of inequalities of race and class. The suppression of workers and the tight surveillance and micromanagement of black and brown lives have always been at the center of policing. Any police reform strategy that does not address this reality is doomed to fail. We must stop looking to procedural reforms and critically evaluate the substantive outcomes of policing. We must constantly reevaluate what the police are asked to do and what impact policing has on the lives of the policed. A kinder, gentler, and more diverse war on the poor is still a war on the poor. As long as the police are tasked with waging simultaneous wars on drugs, crime, disorder, and terrorism, we will have aggressive and invasive policing that disproportionately criminalizes the young, poor, male, and nonwhite.

We are told that the police are the bringers of justice. They are here to help maintain social order so that no one should be subjected to abuse. The neutral enforcement of the law sets us all free. This understanding of policing, however, is largely mythical. Police function, despite whatever good intentions they have, as a tool for managing deeply entrenched inequalities in a way that systematically produces injustices for the poor, socially marginal, and nonwhite.

Part of the problem is that our politicians, media, and criminal justice institutions too often equate justice with revenge. Popular culture is suffused with revenge fantasies in which the aggrieved bring horrible retribution down on those who have hurt them. Often this involves a fantasy of those who have been placed on the margins taking aim at the powerful; it's a fantasy of empowerment through violence. Police and prisons have come to be our preferred tools for inflicting punishment. Our entire criminal justice system has become a gigantic revenge factory. Three-strikes laws, sex-offender registries, the death penalty, and abolishing parole are about retribution, not safety. Whole segments of our society have been deemed always-already guilty. This is not justice; it is oppression. Real justice would look to restore people and communities, to rebuild trust and social cohesion, to offer people a way forward, to reduce the social forces that drive crime, and to treat both victims and perpetrators as full human beings. Our police and larger criminal justice system not only fail at this but rarely see it as even related to their mission.

There are police and other criminal justice agents who want to use their power to improve communities and individuals and protect the "good" people from the "bad" ones. But not all police mean well. Too many engage in abuse based on race, gender, religion, or economic condition. Explicit and intentional racism is alive and well in policing. We are asked to believe that these incidents are the misdeeds of "a few bad apples." But why does the institution of policing so consistently shield these misdeeds? Too often, when biased policing is pointed out, the response is to circle the wagons, deny any intent to do harm, and block any discipline against the officers involved.

This sends an unambiguous message that officers are above the law and free to act on their biases without consequence. It also says that the institution is more concerned about defending itself than rooting out these problems.

Is our society really made safer and more just by incarcerating millions of people? Is asking the police to be the lead agency in dealing with homelessness, mental illness, school discipline, youth unemployment, immigration, youth violence, sex work, and drugs really a way to achieve a better society? Can police really be trained to perform all these tasks in a professional and uncoercive manner?

Any real agenda for police reform must replace police with empowered communities working to solve their own problems. Poor communities of color have suffered the consequences of high crime and disorder. It is their children who are shot and robbed. They have also had to bear the brunt of aggressive, invasive, and humiliating policing. Policing will never be a just or effective tool for community empowerment, much less racial justice. Communities must directly confront the political, economic, and social arrangements that produce the vast gulfs between the races and the growing gaps between the haves and the have-nots. We don't need empty police reforms; we need a robust democracy that gives people the capacity to demand of their government and themselves real, nonpunitive solutions to their problems.

> The problem is not police training, police diversity, or police methods. The problem is the dramatic and unprecedented expansion and intensity of policing in the last forty years, a fundamental shift in the role of police in society. The problem is policing itself.
> **Alex S. Vitale**

The End of Policing

This is an edited excerpt from The End of Policing *by Alex S. Vitale (Verso, 2017).*

SUNDAY NOVEMBER 27

_____

_____

_____

_____

_____

_____

_____

MONDAY NOVEMBER 28

_____

_____

_____

_____

_____

_____

_____

TUESDAY NOVEMBER 29

_____

_____

_____

_____

_____

_____

_____

NOVEMBER 29, 1947 The UN approves the partition of Palestine, despite its rejection by Palestinian Arabs and the fact that 90 percent of privately held land was Arab-owned.

> "They've prohibited oppression among themselves
> but for us they legalized all prohibitions!
> They proclaim, 'Trading with slaves is unlawful'
> but isn't the trading of free people more of a crime?"
>
> —PALESTINIAN POET ABU SALMA, "MY COUNTRY ON PARTITION DAY"

NOVEMBER 30, 1999 The World Trade Organization meeting in Seattle is disrupted by massive anti-globalization protests. "When we smash a window, we aim to destroy the thin veneer of legitimacy that surrounds private property rights." —ACME COLLECTIVE, "ON THE VIOLENCE OF PROPERTY"

DECEMBER 1, 1955 Rosa Parks is arrested for refusing to give up her seat on a segregated bus, which triggers a boycott organized by the Women's Political Council of Montgomery. "Negroes have rights, too, for if Negroes did not ride the busses, they could not operate." —WOMEN'S POLITICAL COUNCIL PAMPHLET

DECEMBER 2, 1964 Berkeley Free Speech Movement leader Mario Savio gives his famous speech on the steps of Sproul Hall. The next day, nearly 800 protesters are arrested on the UC Berkeley campus while resisting restrictions on political speech. "You've got to put your bodies upon the gears and upon the wheels ... upon the levers, upon all the apparatus, and you've got to make it stop."

WEDNESDAY NOVEMBER 30

_____

_____

_____

_____

_____

_____

_____

Rosa Parks (1913–2005) being fingerprinted after her arrest for
boycotting public transportation in Montgomery, Alabama, 1956

THURSDAY DECEMBER 1

_____

_____

_____

_____

_____

_____

_____

NOTES:

_____

_____

_____

_____

_____

_____

FRIDAY DECEMBER 2

_____

_____

_____

_____

_____

_____

SATURDAY DECEMBER 3

_____

_____

_____

_____

_____

_____

SUNDAY DECEMBER 4

_____

_____

_____

_____

_____

_____

_____

MONDAY DECEMBER 5

_____

_____

_____

_____

_____

_____

_____

TUESDAY DECEMBER 6

_____

_____

_____

_____

_____

_____

_____

DECEMBER 4, 1969 Fred Hampton, Black Panther leader, is assassinated in a raid on his apartment by the Chicago Police with the help of the FBI. "We've got to go up on the mountaintop to make this motherfucker understand, goddamnit, that we are coming from the valley!" —HAMPTON SPEECH AT OLIVET CHURCH

DECEMBER 5, 1978 Wei Jingsheng posts his manifesto "The Fifth Modernization," which was critical of the Communist leadership, to Beijing's Democracy Wall, and is imprisoned for 15 years. "Let us find out for ourselves what should be done."

DECEMBER 6, 1928 The United Fruit Company violently suppresses a workers' strike in Colombia, in what becomes known as the Banana Massacre.

DECEMBER 7, 1896 Antonio Maceo, an Afro-Cuban revolutionary, known as the Bronze Titan, dies in the fight for Cuban independence. "Whoever tries to conquer Cuba will gain nothing but the dust of her blood-soaked soil—if he doesn't perish in the struggle first!" —MACEO'S OATH

DECEMBER 9, 2002 To Huu, one of the Viet Minh's most celebrated poets, dies.

"The ditches must go deeper than my hatred.
The work must fly faster than my tears."
—"GUERILLA WOMAN"

DECEMBER 10, 2008 Charter 08, a document for greater democratization, is published, signed by more than 350 Chinese writers, including poet and essayist Woeser, and human rights activist Liu Xiaobo. "The decline of the current system has reached the point where change is no longer optional."

WEDNESDAY DECEMBER 7

_____

_____

_____

_____

_____

_____

_____

Protest in Hong Kong against the arrest of Liu Xiaobo, one of the authors of Charter 08

THURSDAY DECEMBER 8

_____

_____

_____

_____

_____

_____

_____

NOTES:

_____

_____

_____

_____

_____

_____

FRIDAY DECEMBER 9

_____

_____

_____

_____

_____

_____

SATURDAY DECEMBER 10

_____

_____

_____

_____

_____

_____

SUNDAY DECEMBER 11

_____

_____

_____

_____

_____

_____

_____

MONDAY DECEMBER 12

_____

_____

_____

_____

_____

_____

_____

TUESDAY DECEMBER 13

_____

_____

_____

_____

_____

_____

_____

DECEMBER 11, 1977 Moroccan poet Saida Menebhi dies in prison after a thirty-four-day hunger strike. Her work was central in the nationwide attempt to recover the history of the thousands of people who were "disappeared" in the 1970s and 1980s.

"Prison is ugly
you draw it my child
with black marks
for the bars and grills"

DECEMBER 11, 2012 Theresa Spence, Chief of Attawapiskat First Nations in Canada, begins a hunger strike that would set off the indigenous sovereignty movement Idle No More.

DECEMBER 13, 1797 Heinrich Heine, German-Jewish poet and essayist, is born. No writer would be more hated by the Nazis.

"Ye fools, so closely to search my trunk!
Ye will find in it really nothing:
My contraband goods I carry about
In my head, not hid in my clothing"
—"A WINTER'S TALE"

DECEMBER 14, 2008 Iraqi journalist Muntadhar al-Zaidi throws his shoe at US president George W. Bush at a press conference. "This is a farewell kiss from the Iraqi people, you dog."

DECEMBER 16, 1656 Radical English Quaker leader James Nayler is arrested for blasphemy after reenacting Christ's entry into Jerusalem by entering Bristol on a donkey. "There is a spirit which I feel that delights to do no evil, nor to revenge any wrong, but delights to endure all things, in hope to enjoy its own in the end."
—NAYLER'S FINAL STATEMENT

WEDNESDAY DECEMBER 14

Muntadhar al-Zaidi is pulled away after throwing his shoes at George W. Bush

THURSDAY DECEMBER 15

NOTES:

FRIDAY DECEMBER 16

SATURDAY DECEMBER 17

SUNDAY DECEMBER 18

_____

_____

_____

_____

_____

_____

_____

MONDAY DECEMBER 19

_____

_____

_____

_____

_____

_____

_____

TUESDAY DECEMBER 20

_____

_____

_____

_____

_____

_____

_____

DECEMBER 18, 2010 Demonstrations begin in Tunisia, the day after street vendor Mohammed Bouazizi self-immolated in protest of harassment from officials, setting off what would eventually become the Arab Spring.

DECEMBER 19, 1944 US soldier Kurt Vonnegut becomes a Nazi prisoner of war. The experience later shapes his novels, which often explore anti-authoritarian and anti-war themes. "There is no reason goodness cannot triumph over evil, so long as the angels are as organized as the Mafia." —CAT'S CRADLE

DECEMBER 20, 1986 More than 30,000 students march through Shanghai chanting pro-democracy slogans. "When will the people be in charge?"

DECEMBER 23, 1970 After being captured in Bolivia while working as a chronicler for Che Guevara, French journalist Régis Debray is released from prison. "For Che the true difference, the true frontier, is not the one which separates a Bolivian from a Peruvian, a Peruvian from an Argentinian, an Argentinian from a Cuban. It is the one that separates the Latin Americans from the Yankees." —DEBRAY'S TESTIMONY AT HIS COURT-MARTIAL

DECEMBER 23, 1986 Dissident and Nobel Peace Prize–winner Andrei Sakharov returns to Moscow after six years spent in internal exile for protesting the Soviet war in Afghanistan. "Freedom of thought is the only guarantee against an infection of people by mass myths, which, in the hands of treacherous hypocrites and demagogues, can be transformed into bloody dictatorship."

WEDNESDAY DECEMBER 21

Demonstrators face police lines on Aveunue Bourguiba, Central Tunis, 2011

THURSDAY DECEMBER 22

NOTES:

FRIDAY DECEMBER 23

SATURDAY DECEMBER 24

SUNDAY DECEMBER 25

_____

_____

_____

_____

_____

_____

_____

MONDAY DECEMBER 26

_____

_____

_____

_____

_____

_____

_____

TUESDAY DECEMBER 27

_____

_____

_____

_____

_____

_____

_____

DECEMBER 25, 1831 Samuel Sharpe, leader of the Native Baptists of Montego Bay, leads Jamaican slaves in the Great Jamaican Slave Revolt, which was instrumental in abolishing chattel slavery. "I would rather die upon yonder gallows than live in slavery." —SHARPE'S LAST WORDS

DECEMBER 25, 1927 B. R. Ambedkar, an architect of the Indian constitution who was born into the Dalit caste of "untouchables," leads followers to burn the Manusmriti, an ancient text justifying the hierarchy. The "untouchables" were relegated to occupations considered impure, like butchering and waste removal.

DECEMBER 25, 1977 Domitila Barrios de Chungara, an activist with the militant Bolivian labor group Housewives' Committee, begins a hunger strike that leads to the end of the US-backed Bolivian dictatorship. "The first battle to be won is to let the woman, the man, the children participate in the struggle of the working class, so that the home can become a stronghold that the enemy can't overcome."

DECEMBER 30, 1884 William Morris, Eleanor Marx, and others establish the Socialist League, a revolutionary organization in the UK. "Civilization has reduced the workman to such a skinny and pitiful existence, that he scarcely knows how to frame a desire for any life much better." —MORRIS, "HOW I BECAME A SOCIALIST"

DECEMBER 31, 1977 Kenyan writer Ngũgĩ wa Thiong'o is imprisoned for cowriting a play critical of the Kenyan government.

> "We the workers in factories and plantations said in one voice:
> We reject slave wages!
> Do you remember the 1948 general strike?"
> —NGŨGĨ WA THIONG'O AND NGŨGĨ WA MIRII, _I WILL MARRY WHEN I WANT_

WEDNESDAY DECEMBER 28

B. R. Ambedkar during his tenure as chairman of the committee for drafting the constitution, 1950

THURSDAY DECEMBER 29

NOTES:

FRIDAY DECEMBER 30

SATURDAY DECEMBER 31

VERSO READING LISTS

RADICAL HISTORIES

**INSURGENT EMPIRE: ANTICOLONIALISM
AND THE MAKING OF BRITISH DISSENT**
PRIYAMVADA GOPAL

**THE COMMON WIND: AFRO-AMERICAN
CURRENTS IN THE AGE OF THE HAITIAN
REVOLUTION**
JULIUS S SCOTT.

SET THE NIGHT ON FIRE: L.A. IN THE SIXTIES
MIKE DAVIS AND JON WIENER

**A WORLD TO WIN:
THE LIFE AND WORKS OF KARL MARX**
SVEN-ERIC LIEDMAN

**OCTOBER: THE STORY OF
THE RUSSIAN REVOLUTION**
CHINA MIÉVILLE

**THE AMERICAN CRUCIBLE: SLAVERY,
EMANCIPATION AND HUMAN RIGHTS**
ROBIN BLACKBURN

LINEAGES OF THE ABSOLUTIST STATE
PERRY ANDERSON

ECOLOGY AND CLIMATE CHANGE

**HOW TO BLOW UP A PIPELINE:
LEARNING TO FIGHT IN A WORLD ON FIRE**
ANDREAS MALM

THE CASE FOR THE GREEN NEW DEAL
ANN PETTIFOR

**A PLANET TO WIN:
WHY WE NEED A GREEN NEW DEAL**
KATE ARONOFF, ALYSSA BATTISTONI, ET AL.

**THE CLIMATE CRISIS AND THE GLOBAL GREEN
NEW DEAL: THE POLITICAL ECONOMY OF
SAVING THE PLANET**
NOAM CHOMSKY AND ROBERT POLLIN

**PLANET ON FIRE:
A MANIFESTO FOR THE AGE OF
ENVIRONMENTAL BREAKDOWN**

**FOSSIL CAPITAL: THE RISE OF STEAM POWER
AND THE ROOTS OF GLOBAL WARMING**
ANDREAS MALM

WORK AND AUTOMATION

**INVENTING THE FUTURE:
POSTCAPITALISM AND A WORLD
WITHOUT WORK**
NICK SRNICEK AND ALEX WILLIAMS

AUTOMATION AND THE FUTURE OF WORK
AARON BENANAV

**OVERTIME:
WHY WE NEED A SHORTER WORKING WEEK**
KYLE LEWIS AND WILL STRONG

WHY YOU SHOULD BE A TRADE UNIONIST
LEN McCLUSKEY

**FULLY AUTOMATED LUXURY COMMUNISM:
A MANIFESTO**
AARON BASTANI

FEMINISM AND GENDER

THE VERSO BOOK OF FEMINISM: REVOLUTIONARY WORDS FROM FOUR MILLENNIA OF REBELLION
EDITED BY JESSIE KINDIG

GLITCH FEMINISM
LEGACY RUSSELL

FEMALES
ANDREA LONG CHU

FEMINISM FOR THE 99%: A MANIFESTO
CINZIA ARRUZZA, TITHI BHATTACHARYA AND NANCY FRASER

BURN IT DOWN! FEMINIST MANIFESTOS FOR THE REVOLUTION
EDITED BY BREANNE FAHS

REVOLTING PROSTITUTES: THE FIGHT FOR SEX-WORKERS' RIGHTS
MOLLY SMITH AND JUNO MAC

FEMINISM AND NATIONALISM IN THE THIRD WORLD
KUMARI JAYAWARDENA

ECONOMICS

THE NEW SPIRIT OF CAPITALISM
LUC BOLTANSKI AND EVE CHIAPELLO

THE PRODUCTION OF MONEY: HOW TO BREAK THE POWER OF BANKERS
ANN PETTIFOR

THE COMPLETE WORKS OF ROSA LUXEMBURG, VOLUME II: ECONOMIC WRITINGS 2
ROSA LUXEMBURG

A COMPANION TO MARX'S CAPITAL, VOLUME 1 AND VOLUME 2
DAVID HARVEY

FORTUNES OF FEMINISM: FROM STATE-MANAGED CAPITALISM TO NEOLIBERAL CRISIS
NANCY FRASER

RACE AND ETHNICITY

FUTURES OF BLACK RADICALISM
EDITED BY GAYE THERESA JOHNSON AND ALEX LUBIN

A KICK IN THE BELLY: WOMEN, SLAVERY AND RESISTANCE
STELLA DADZIE

IF THEY COME IN THE MORNING … : VOICES OF RESISTANCE
EDITED BY ANGELA Y. DAVIS

RACECRAFT: THE SOUL OF INEQUALITY IN AMERICAN LIFE
KAREN E. FIELDS AND BARBARA J. FIELDS

HOW EUROPE UNDERDEVELOPED AFRICA
WALTER RODNEY

BEYOND BLACK AND WHITE: FROM CIVIL RIGHTS TO BARACK OBAMA
MANNING MARABLE

ACTIVISM AND RESISTANCE

THE VERSO BOOK OF DISSENT: REVOLUTIONARY WORDS FROM THREE MILLENNIA OF REBELLION AND RESISTANCE
EDITED BY ANDREW HSIAO AND AUDREA LIM

THE END OF POLICING
ALEX S. VITALE

OUR HISTORY IS THE FUTURE: STANDING ROCK VERSUS THE DAKOTA ACCESS PIPELINE, AND THE LONG TRADITION OF INDIGENOUS RESISTANCE
NICK ESTES

DIRECT ACTION: PROTEST AND THE REINVENTION OF AMERICAN RADICALISM
L.A. KAUFFMAN

POLICING THE PLANET: WHY THE POLICING CRISIS LED TO BLACK LIVES MATTER
EDITED BY JORDAN T. CAMP AND CHRISTINA HEATHERTON

ART AND AESTHETICS

**ARTIFICIAL HELLS: PARTICIPATORY ART
AND THE POLITICS OF SPECTATORSHIP**
CLAIRE BISHOP

SAVAGE MESSIAH
LAURA GRACE FORD

**ALL THAT IS SOLID MELTS INTO AIR:
THE EXPERIENCE OF MODERNITY**
MARSHALL BERMAN

PORTRAITS: JOHN BERGER ON ARTISTS
JOHN BERGER

**AISTHESIS: SCENES FROM
THE AESTHETIC REGIME OF ART**
JACQUES RANCIÈRE

CITIES AND ARCHITECTURE

**FEMINIST CITY:
CLAIMING SPACE IN A MAN-MADE WORLD**
LESLIE KERN

**MUNICIPAL DREAMS:
THE RISE AND FALL OF COUNCIL HOUSING**
JOHN BOUGHTON

**EXTRASTATECRAFT:
THE POWER OF INFASTRUCTURE SPACE**
KELLER EASTERLING

**CAPITAL CITY:
GENTRIFICATION AND THE REAL ESTATE STATE**
SAMUEL STEIN

**REBEL CITIES: FROM THE RIGHT TO THE CITY
TO THE URBAN REVOLUTION**
DAVID HARVEY

PHILOSOPHY AND THEORY

**THE FORCE OF NONVIOLENCE:
THE ETHICAL IN THE POLITICAL**
JUDITH BUTLER

**THE LEFT HEMISPHERE:
MAPPING CRITICAL THEORY TODAY**
RAZMIG KEUCHEYAN

CRITIQUE OF EVERYDAY LIFE
HENRI LEFEBVRE

**MINIMA MORALIA:
REFLECTIONS FROM DAMAGED LIFE**
THEODOR ADORNO

NO WALLS, NO BORDERS

**THE DISPOSSESSED: A STORY OF ASYLUM
AT THE US–MEXICAN BORDER AND BEYOND**
JOHN WASHINGTON

**HOSTILE ENVIRONMENT:
HOW IMMIGRANTS BECAME SCAPEGOATS**
MAYA GOODFELLOW

**ALL-AMERICAN NATIVISM: HOW THE BIPARTISAN WA
ON IMMIGRANTS EXPLAINS POLITICS AS WE KNOW I**
DANIEL DENVIR

**WE BUILT THE WALL:
HOW THE US KEEPS OUT ASYLUM SEEKERS FROM
MEXICO, CENTRAL AMERICA AND BEYOND**
EILEEN TRUAX

**VIOLENT BORDERS:
REFUGEES AND THE RIGHT TO MOVE**
REECE JONES

POLITICAL THEORY

**THE OLD IS DYING AND THE NEW CANNOT BE
BORN: FROM PROGRESSIVE NEOLIBERALISM
TO TRUMP AND BEYOND**
NANCY FRASER WITH BHASKAR SUNKARA

**HOW TO BE AN ANTICAPITALIST IN THE
TWENTY-FIRST CENTURY**
ERIK OLIN WRIGHT

**DEMOCRACY AGAINST CAPITALISM:
RENEWING HISTORICAL MATERIALISM**
ELLEN MEISKINS WOOD

**IMAGINED COMMUNITIES: REFLECTIONS ON
THE ORIGIN AND SPREAD OF NATIONALISM**
BENEDICT ANDERSON

FOR A LEFT POPULISM
CHANTAL MOUFFE